QUEEN PIN

QUEEN PIN

JEMEKER THOMPSON-HAIRSTON
WITH DAVID RITZ

GRAND CENTRAL PUBLISHING

New York Boston

Grand Central Publishing
Hachette Book Group
1290 Avenue of the Americas
New York, NY 10104

www.HachetteBookGroup.com

First Edition: June 2010

Grand Central Publishing is a division of Hachette Book Group, Inc.
The Grand Central Publishing name and logo is a trademark of Hachette Book Group, Inc.

Library of Congress Cataloging-in-Publication Data

Thompson-Hairston, Jemeker.
Queen pin / Jemeker Thompson-Hairston; with David Ritz.—1st ed.
p. cm.
ISBN 978-0-446-54288-3
1. Thompson-Hairston, Jemeker. 2. Women drug dealers—United States—Biography. 3. Criminals—Rehabilitation—United States—Biography. I. Ritz, David. II. Title.
HV5805.T496A3 2010
363.45092—dc22
2009046972

THIS BOOK IS DEDICATED FIRST TO MY LORD AND SAVIOR JESUS CHRIST, AND TO THE MEMORY OF MY PRECIOUS GRANDPARENTS, MR. AND MRS. WILLIE GEORGE; ELIZABETH RICHARDSON; MY FATHER, WILLIE FRANK THOMPSON; AND MY BROTHER, ANTHONY RAY JOHNSON.

TO MY HUSBAND, ROD (CHAMP) HAIRSTON, WHO IS MY SUPPORT AND STRENGTH. BEING UNITED WITH YOU HAS BEEN ONE OF MY GREATEST BLESSINGS. IT HAS BEEN SO COMFORTING TO WATCH YOU GROW, IN GOD'S GRACE, AS THE HEAD OF OUR FAMILY.

INTRODUCTION

As I tell you this story, I'm not the person I was. The woman I'm about to describe no longer exists. She is a character from a different time and a different place. But there's no way around it: she is me, and the story is mine.

I have to own it. I have to tell it. I have to relive it in a way that makes sense out of the mess—the violence, mayhem, and tragedy—that became my life.

God has dealt with me in ways I could never have anticipated. I would not have become the person I am today without twelve hard years in prison. And to be honest, part of me doesn't want to look back at the death and destruction caused by my hand as a drug dealer and a known operator whose notoriety and success rivaled the most powerful men. In being true to the God who loved me enough to save me from myself, though, I must make this public confession.

It is the testimony of who I was and what I did, what happened to me, and who I am today.

Nothing more, nothing less.

WANTED

There's nothing better to start my day than a bubble bath.

A warm bubble bath always clears my head and calms my nerves. As long as I'm in the tub, my body is relaxed, my mind calm, my emotions at ease, and my soul at peace. I'm on the top floor of a luxury South Beach Miami hotel, overlooking the beautiful turquoise blue of the ocean.

Last night, I ended up with a man whose bed I left just hours ago—a one-night stand with one of the Kansas City Chiefs. I don't care if I ever hear from him again. Last night wasn't about him, it was all about me.

Suddenly the phone rings.

I jump.

My eyes open and my stomach feels ill.

I used to be happy when the phone rang. A ringing phone meant business was good. Now it makes me wonder if *they* know where I am.

I'm alone and confused and unwilling to admit it. I'm not living in the deepest part of my mind. Instead, I'm living on the surface and skating over thin ice. I'm holding on to control because *they've* been chasing me. I've been running so that I can't be caught. Being caught is not an option. There are no mistakes allowed. *They* can make mistakes. *But I can't.* As long as I stay in control, I keep my freedom.

I listen to the phone ring. Could be the front desk and could be the Feds. All I know is that *no one* should be calling me here. So much for relaxation; my therapy session is over.

I climb out of the tub and begin to dress myself: Bob Mackie suit, Maud Frizon pumps, gold Rolex, diamond tennis bracelet, imported Italian wig. Everything that I'm not wearing is packed and ready to go.

The phone continues to ring and the gears in my head continue to turn.

If it's the front desk calling, they don't know I'm in this room. If it's somebody else, I don't know what they know.

I have several aliases, each with a matching ID and credit card: Jann Quinn, Wanda Jones, Lisa Jones, and the one I've got with me—Tami Jones. The IDs say everything but Jemeker Mosley, whom the FBI wants for conspiracy to distribute cocaine, money laundering, and I don't know what else.

I know what I've done.

If *they* know, it means life without parole.

I'm not going out like that. They'll have to kill me to catch me.

One thing at a time, I tell myself. *Get it together. Make it to the airport. Keep moving. The important thing is not to panic.*

I grab the rest of my belongings from the nightstand but the last item stops me cold. It's a photograph of a happy, smiling nine-year-old boy. He looks just like Jane, Tami, Wanda, Lisa, and Jemeker. It's the only thing they all have in common—a beautiful son named Anthony.

Seeing his picture takes me back to happier times. Back to before *they* were chasing me. The memories flood my mind—the first time Anthony called me "Mama," his first birthday party, the first time my baby told me he loved me.

Get it together, Jemeker.

I usually don't mix what I feel and what I do. But when I see my baby, it's difficult—I haven't held him in my arms in six months. We used to be inseparable—wherever I went, he went. Now he stays with my mother, where he can go to school and have a normal life, not like mine. But Lord knows I miss my son.

When I call, it always ends the same:

"I miss you, Mom."

"I miss you too, baby. And I'll be there soon."

"That's what you said last time—when you said you'd come to Granny's for Christmas. Then it was Easter. When are you coming home?"

By the time he's in tears, I'm asking myself how I'll ever make it up to him. I can live with everything I've done except for this.

But Jemeker can't go home.

Once a week, the Feds case the office where Jemeker built up her hair business. They can't open the books or the cash box because it's a legitimate company, but they can stake it out, which is exactly what they do. And when they aren't doing that, they're at my mother's house, harassing her as well.

"Where's your daughter, Missus Johnson?"

"I don't know. Same as the last time you came around."

"Do you know that your daughter is one of the biggest cocaine dealers in America?"

That's the message my mother relays when I call her. She says that the Feds are asking about me.

"And what did you say?"

"The truth. I don't know your business."

"Did you get the money I sent?" I ask.

"Yeah."

It's quiet for a moment. "Anthony's sixth grade graduation is the day after tomorrow," she says, then adds, "He wants you to be there."

I could keep running forever.

That's what I think ten minutes after I hang up the phone. I could keep changing my identity as long as necessary. I have friends, connections, and unlimited money. As long as I'm still Jemeker from the Game, I'll always be a queen. I could even walk out of my life and never look back. I could forget about everything and everyone I've ever known and run. But then I reach in my purse and look at my baby's picture and that notion evaporates. I have a moment of clarity.

I'm separated from my son. He doesn't understand why. I know the embarrassment and shame he feels because my mom tells me so. I've been selfish, trying to control my life, even if it means I might ruin Anthony's. It's just too much. I know the risk if I show up, but it's worth it for my son.

I call a cab and go to the airport.

The lady behind the counter asks me where I'd like to go.

Tami hands over her credit card.

"Los Angeles, please."

Jemeker is going home.

Six hours later, I'm back in Los Angeles, safe in a town house I keep in Westchester. It's not much to look at from the outside—and you'll never see me coming or going through the front door—but the inside is laid out. I lock the dead bolts, set the alarm, and draw the shades.

I'm safe for the moment.

Remember why you're here.

I start thinking about what needs to be done. Lisa Jones wants to pay the car note, rent, and utilities. Jane Quinn wants to work out. At the gym, just when she's about to complete her workout on the sit-up bench, a man asks, "How many sets do you have left?"

"I've just started."

"Mind if my friends and I work in?"

"Not at all."

Three gentlemen and I take turns using the bench. When we are through, they invite me to lunch. It turns out they are all police officers. It might sound like I'm playing with fire, but I'm not nervous. I feel safe among my new friends, knowing that this is the last place the Feds will look for me.

Back at my apartment, I take a nap to clear my head and fall into a dream. I'm not normally a dreamer and I don't remember them when they happen, but this one is different. Actually, it doesn't feel like a dream at all—it looks and feels like real life.

I'm at the gym. I'm working out. Working hard to work through my problems, like lifting weights will clear my head again. Except the harder I try, the harder it is to concentrate.

Did I tell the cops I was Lisa or Jane?

Which days do I work out?

What day is it today?

What do I do after this workout?

I wake up and try to shake the dream—forget the

gym, the police, and whatever day it is. I can always run again.

Again, remember why you're here, Jemeker.

The graduation is tomorrow. That still leaves tonight to party. I call my friend Sumer—we go all the way back to high school—and my younger brother Fernando and tell them we're going out tonight.

Sumer shows up with Fernando around eleven thirty. She's smart about it: she drives around the block three times to make sure nobody's following, then pulls in the alley and pages me on my beeper. I walk out the back and get in the passenger seat and we drive off.

On the way downtown to a club called Safe Sex, I tell Fernando, "Pass me the Hennessy bottle and the joint."

Fernando is shocked. I don't *ever* drink or smoke. But tonight I don't care.

Even when I'm high and drunk, I can't stop thinking about my baby. His first wobbly steps. His first birthday party at the house on Fifty-fourth and Western—where I turned the whole yard into a carnival. His first graduation from preschool. The first time he called me "Mama."

I try to control my thoughts to escape those familiar feelings of pain.

My mind is still spinning when we arrive at the club.

"Girl, look at this line," Sumer says. "Do what you do."

We walk to the front, past the players, hustlers, and wannabes. Some I recognize. Some I don't. But they all know me. When we hit the door, the head bouncer simply peels the velvet rope back. I don't have to say a word.

Once inside, I numb the memories of everything I'm trying to forget. Hours later, I choose a Mr. Right Now to go home with. Sumer follows me to his place. I'm not there long. I don't know if he got his, but I got mine, and that's all that matters.

This time, when I return home and fall asleep, I don't dream.

I come around the next morning at nine thirty. Graduation's at ten thirty.

Hold it together, Jemeker. Come up with a plan: 1. Take a shower. 2. Get to the school by noon to catch the end of the ceremony. 3. Take Anthony to Benihana. 4. Hit the road again by nighttime...maybe Vegas, maybe Detroit, maybe back to Miami, maybe Atlanta.

After my shower I pick out a black linen Donna Karan dress—nothing flashy. I think twice about wearing a wig and decide against it, choosing some gold-rimmed Chanel glasses with extra dark lenses instead. Then I go to the flower shop, where I pick out two dozen yellow roses for Anthony.

On the way to school, I pray: *God, let everything go smooth today. Don't let any of my wrongs affect my son. Whatever happens, watch over and protect us.*

God has always had my back.

I'm the most blessed lady I know.

But even with my prayer, my heart's hammering inside my chest. I'm so close to seeing my baby. I've still got both eyes peeled for police, Feds, helicopters, anyone following me. Can't slip now. I am not making any mistakes today, June 29, 1993.

I have to see Anthony.

I need to hold my baby in my arms.

I get to Cowan Elementary at noon. I park in front of the school and walk toward the auditorium, keeping my head down. The graduation's over and there are kids and parents out front.

Everything's going to be fine...

I can't see Anthony but he sees me.

"Mom!" he yells.

I hear my baby's voice...

But as soon as I turn my head, a strong hand grabs my left arm. I look up to see a handsome light-skinned man with nice hair, dressed like a distinguished gentleman.

"Come quietly," he says as he walks me back toward the street. "There's a lot of kids here."

He's so smooth in his approach, he might as well be my escort. But my heart stops cold and falls into the pit of my stomach.

It's *them.*

I look back, lock eyes with Sumer's, and wave her off with my right hand. She knows exactly what I mean: *Don't come near me, girl. Go get Anthony. Don't let my son see this.*

Soon as we get to the curb, another agent in a tweed coat takes my other arm.

This is it.

I look into my son's eyes and know what he's thinking:

Mommy's being arrested.

They walk me down the block, around the corner, and out of sight. Undercover police are coming out of the woodwork. Anthony, Sumer, and Mama Lera, Sumer's mother, follow at a distance. Sumer takes my baby in her arms. She tries to calm him down but it's no use. All three of them are crying.

Suddenly, I remember I have five thousand dollars, the keys to my car, Jane's ID, and a couple credit cards in my purse.

The ID and the cards are another case.

I throw it to Mama Lera.

A policeman dressed like a janitor goes after the purse. Mama Lera clutches it to her chest and starts screaming at him: *"You ain't getting this purse!!"* The janitor threatens to arrest her and she screams, *"Then we're ALL gonna go to jail!!"* After that, she's on a roll: *"You don't know who she is!"* and *"She didn't do nothing!"* and

"Y'all can't do this!" and a whole lot of other stuff a lady shouldn't say. She's yelling so loud and cussing so bad in her island patois, I wonder if they're going to arrest her too.

She doesn't know what's going on.

The handsome light-skinned agent tells the janitor to let the purse go. I ask him if I can say good-bye to Anthony. He says yes. I move to take my son in my arms.

Got him.

"I'm so proud of you," I whisper softly.

I will not cry.

Jemeker, you WILL not cry in front of your son, these police, or anyone else.

"You made it," he says. Holding my baby feels so good, I don't ever want to let him go. For this one moment, everything's okay.

But then I feel the handsome light-skinned agent's hand on my shoulder again. "It's time to go, Missus Mosley."

I'm still staring at my baby's face as they take me back and read me my rights. Feels like I'm dreaming again. I can't take my eyes off Anthony as he starts screaming, *"I want my mommy!! I want my mommy!!"* and he won't stop looking at me. My lips move—*I'm sorry, baby, I'm so sorry*—but they don't make any sound. My guts turn inside out. I feel dead.

The Feds hustle me into the back seat of a government car. Sumer yells something about calling a lawyer as they shut the door. I toss and turn to look behind me as the car pulls away from the curb. I can see the tears streaming down my baby's cheeks.

I'm numb.

PART I

BEFORE THE GAME

EVICTED

When I was eight years old, spring arrived early. I remember coming home from school one day to the sound of the baby birds crying in the trees, crying so loudly I knew something was wrong. In my little-girl mind, I imagined those baby birds were crying for their mommy to come home and make everything okay.

Looking back, I think I was scared my mother could not take care of me. It was easy to think, especially on that afternoon in May when me and my three brothers were standing in front of the little house on Sycamore Avenue that our mother rented. We were standing there because we had been evicted.

The sun was shining and the baby birds were crying their hearts out up in the big avocado tree behind our house. As a crew of workers carried our stuff out the front door, the man who owned the house fired up a chain saw to trim that tree and clean the property up for somebody else.

I just stood there, listening and watching. An old car sputtered by. Across the street, a squeaky screen door kept opening and slapping shut. Neighbors came by and stared but no one offered to help. At one point, I saw my friend Connie's mother look into my eyes, then look away, like there was nothing she could do. Like she was afraid we were going to ask her for help. I could see the fear and humiliation in her eyes, but she wasn't the one out on the curb.

"Where's your mom?" she asked me.

"At work," I replied.

"Help me! Help me!" I imagined the baby birds saying over the chain saw. Were they going to lose their home too? Something told me they could cry all they wanted but it was no use. Just like them, there wasn't anything I could do.

Standing out there, exposed and ashamed, we might as well have had a sign over our heads that read Homeless. By now, the movers had put everything we owned out on the lawn: the furniture my mom and dad used to have card parties with. The dishes my brothers and I used for meals. The TV we used to watch Saturday morning cartoons—where would we plug it in now? The record player, my little pink bike with the white basket, all my toys...even my favorite dress draped over the rosebush with the newly blossomed little yellow buds.

Everything.

The note on the door said it all: Immediate Eviction.

I guess Mom didn't have the money to pay the rent. I stood out there, naked to the world, hearing those little babies crying, *"Help me! Help me!"* and thought about them in that big avocado tree. I wondered if they had family they could stay with. I wondered if their mother could find them another place to live. I wondered if she would get back to them before the man with the chain saw did. Where *was* their mom? Was she out trying to get them food? Did she know *they* were being evicted? Was she going to save her babies?

I flat out hated the whole thing. Hated not knowing where we were going to go, hated not knowing what we were going to do next. Hated not being able to do anything about it. Hated knowing my mom worked so hard and we still didn't have enough.

HOMELESS

"Don't tell your daddy about this," Mom said when she finally got home. "You hear me? Not a word."

I knew one thing for sure, standing out there in front of what used to be our house. This wasn't okay, I wanted to be okay in a bad, bad way.

My mom, Lonnie Johnson, had left my dad, Willie Frank Thompson, when I was four. She caught him with a white lady he'd been seeing on the side and moved out with me and my three brothers, Tony, Johnny, and Fernando. We bumped around a few places before she found the little house over on Sycamore Avenue, near Baldwin Hills, in Los Angeles. For a while things were almost okay. Sycamore Avenue was quiet and shady, and you could play in the middle of the street. I had some friends, like Debbie and Connie, who walked the five blocks to Cienega Elementary School every morning, just like me.

But Debbie and Connie had families with parents who were together. Why not me? Why couldn't my parents work it out? Whenever I asked my mom if she still loved my dad, she'd tell me not to be silly, but it didn't make sense. If she still loved him, why weren't they together? Even if she didn't love him, why couldn't she ask him for help, just to get us out of this mess?

"Why can't we go stay with my dad?" I said back at the curb.

Even if my parents weren't together anymore, sometimes Dad still came around and did things with us. I loved it when we were together—laughing and joking like we were still a real family—and thought maybe we could be like that again. That day, my idea sounded pretty good, whether Mom said so or not.

"Your dad has his own problems," Mom yelled, "and he doesn't need to know what goes on under my roof."

We don't have a roof, I thought to myself.

"That's not his business," she continued. "Stay here with your brothers while I handle this."

Stay here while I handle this. Mom said that all the time. I could see that she worked hard, but it seemed like she was running just to stand still. Even to me, that didn't make sense. Grown-ups were always telling us kids to work hard at everything...and Mom worked hard, no question. But if she worked so hard, how come we were out on the street?

It was even more confusing, considering Mom's job.

She was in the air force reserves and was also a probation officer for the California Youth Authority—people counted on her to watch over delinquents and foster kids—but why didn't they pay her enough to take care of her own kids? I was confused and angry and the whole thing made my stomach twist up in knots.

Back out on the lawn, on that May afternoon, Mom disappeared only to return an hour later with a U-Haul truck and told us to start loading. It took us a number of trips to her friend's garage and it was almost dark by the time we finished. By then, everyone was hungry and tired, and I still didn't know where I was going to lay my head that night. Hungry, tired, or whatever it was, the knots in my stomach twisted tighter and the more they turned, the madder I became.

"Where are we going to eat?" I asked when none of my brothers did. One more time, Mom told me to be quiet. When Tony and Johnny said it, we stopped at McDonald's. Seemed like when one of the boys said something, she did it.

Mom stopped at three different pay phones while we sat in the car eating hamburgers and fries. Nobody said anything. Maybe they were okay, but I wanted to be back in *my* room, in *my* bed, knowing that in the morning when I woke up, I was going to walk to *my* school with *my* friends.

"What's Mom doing?" I asked out loud.

"I don't know," said Tony.

"I don't care," said Johnny.

"You don't care where we're sleeping tonight?" I asked. They looked at each other but didn't say anything. Whether they cared or not, it was clear they weren't thinking like I was.

"Why'd we get kicked out?"

"'Cause Mom didn't pay the rent," Johnny said.

"Why didn't she pay the rent?"

"'Cause she didn't have the money," he continued.

"Why didn't she have the money?"

"'Cause they don't pay her enough."

There it was. *Them. They.* Who were *they*? Didn't they care if we had a place to live? And if they didn't care, who was going to take care of us? The whole thing had me confused, angry, and scared.

After what seemed like forever, Mom got back in the car. I was about to open my mouth again and ask more questions, but I could tell she was upset. This looked bad. And when we finally got where we were going, I understood why.

At least we were off the street.

At least we didn't have to sleep in the car.

At least we were together.

We ended up at the West Adams Manor because it was the only place my mom could find. It was hard to tell what it was like in the dark, but when Mom got the keys and turned on the lights, there were two beds, a black-and-white TV, a beat-up old table, two chairs, and a tiny bathroom... for the five of us.

The feeling I had in the car that told me to be quiet had followed us as we entered the room. It hung in the air like the stale cigarette smell on the sheets and towels—sheets and towels that were nowhere near as soft as Mom's. As we settled in to our new home, nobody said a word.

We were dead tired. My stomach was still twisted in knots and I wanted some of that pink stuff Mom gave me when I had a tummy ache. It looked like she needed some too, but I wasn't about to say anything. I hadn't ever seen Mom like this. Mom always had everything under control. Mom never complained—whatever she was going through, she didn't show it. But this was different.

The boys slept in one bed.

Me and Mom slept in the other one.

I was grateful we had a place to sleep. But I didn't sleep much. Never mind the sound of Mom crying in the bathroom after she thought we were asleep. Never mind the sound of the leaky faucet. I couldn't turn off my mind.

What if we had to stay here for the rest of our lives?

What if it never got any better than this?

The next morning I woke up, cleaned up, got dressed, and walked back to my old block before meeting Connie and Debbie, just like normal. Everybody might have known we'd been evicted, but I wasn't going to let anybody—least of all my two friends—see me walking from where we were staying now.

That's how it went for the next month. I started asking Mom, "How long do we have to be here?" and saying, "I want my old bedroom back." She'd tell me to be quiet, but I knew I wanted to live in a house. Being here was starting to feel like being on punishment. Living at the motel made me feel like the walls were starting to close in.

Third grade was almost over and summer vacation just around the corner, but every morning was the same routine. Every morning on that walk back to where I used to live, I thought the same thing: *What could I do?* With no money and no job, how was an eight-year-old girl supposed to do anything about anything? Somehow I was going to find an answer. Somehow I was going to do something about this.

One afternoon, I was coming out of the motel and Debbie and her dad pulled up to the local market across the street. They saw me. I saw them. Then I saw them eyeing the motel.

"Why are you staying *there?*" Debbie said.

I couldn't even talk, I was so embarrassed.

"That's none of your business," Debbie's daddy said, grabbed her arm, and dragged her into the market. But I could see the look in his eyes as they walked away—it was the same one as on Connie's mom's face the day we were evicted. After a few minutes of standing there and feeling like a fool, an idea—a great idea, an idea I came up with all on my own—lit up my brain.

"Mom," I said after she came home, "where does *your* mom stay?"

"Hattiesburg, Mississippi," she told me.

"Does she have a house?"

"Yes," Mom said.

"Well, I want to go stay with *her*."

It wasn't a request and it wasn't a suggestion. It was a fact. In my mind, I had just told my mother how it was going to be. I didn't know my grandmother and Mom didn't talk about her much. I didn't even know where Mississippi was or what to expect. But there it was—a way out.

Mom didn't argue.

And the day after school was out, off I went.

MUH'DEAR

I knew three things about Hattiesburg as I rode the plane that took me there. First, it was in Mississippi. Second, it was where my grandmother lived. Third, it had to be better than Los Angeles, since being in Los Angeles meant being in that motel.

I had asked my mom about her mom before I left. I wanted to know what she was like and why she didn't ever talk about her.

"Be good" was all Mom told me. "Mind your grandmother and do what she tells you. Muh'Dear doesn't play."

"Muh'Dear?" I asked.

"Muh'Dear," she said, pronouncing it with a southern drawl I'd never heard in her voice. "That's what you call her, Jemeker."

"That's what *you* call her?" I asked.

"That's what everybody calls her."

"*Everybody?*" I pressed. "Everybody in all of Mississippi?"

"*Everybody,*" Mom said, serious all of a sudden. "Your granddaddy, your aunties and uncles, your cousins... everybody. Muh'Dear's who she is."

I hadn't ever heard her talk that way about anybody before—almost like she was scared.

"Is she mean?" I asked.

"She's Muh'Dear," Mom said. "You'll see."

Soon as I got off that plane, I could see Hattiesburg was nothing like Los Angeles. Hattiesburg was small. Hattiesburg was country. Moisture was heavy in the air and it smelled like fresh-cut grass. Even at the airport, this place sounded like crickets and birds instead of cars and people. As for the people, they weren't dressed like L.A. folks. They said "hi" when they passed instead of looking each other up and down.

Someone was looking me up and down, though. Waiting at the edge of the blacktop was a great big woman in a floral print dress and matching hat. Her deep black skin glistened in the sun.

Muh'Dear.

Soon as our eyes met she began strutting toward me. When she was at arm's length, my grandmother grabbed me in a hug and sized me up.

"So this is Lonnie C.'s girl," she clucked. "Light-skinned like your mama...skinny too...has she been feedin' you, child?"

"Yeah," I mumbled.

Big mistake.

I don't know which came first—my grandmother's face dropping or the slap against the back of my head. But as soon as she hit me she had my complete attention.

"No disrespect down here," she said. "Understand?"

"Yes," I mumbled.

"Yes *what?*" she asked.

Before I could respond, I felt her hand against my head again. I couldn't believe it: my mom had *never* hit me even once and here my grandmother had just done it twice!

"Uh-uh. It's 'Yes, ma'am,' and 'No, ma'am.'"

For once, I was silent.

"You're spoiled," she went on, tsking through her teeth. "Lonnie C. spoiled you rotten. But you ain't gonna be a brat down here. You may run your mama but you don't run me."

Standing there, fresh off that plane, farther from home than I'd ever been in my whole life, I was already scared to death of my grandmother.

"Your uncle Roy's waitin' on us," Muh'Dear said, pointing at the parking lot. "C'mon. Let's go home."

Home.

"Yes, ma'am," I responded.

I might have been scared, but I still felt like I was supposed to be there. Hattiesburg was safe. Family in Mississippi wasn't like family in Los Angeles. Here in Muh'Dear's four-bedroom, one-story brick house, there were eleven of us, and that was without any cousins or Muh'Dear's older children over for supper. Still, I slept easy, knowing the roof over my head was bought and paid for and everything ran according to schedule. Muh'Dear got her family together at mealtime, paid the light bill when it was due, made sure everyone went to school, and helped the neighbors whenever they needed it.

During the summer of 1971, I made friends with a girl named Tynia, who also had a big family in a big house...and I loved being in the middle of their business too.

In Hattiesburg, everybody knew your business. If I walked home from Tynia's house and didn't say "Good morning, Miss Ellie," or "Good evening, Mister Willie," word got back faster than I did. And when I *did* get home, Muh'Dear made me retrace my steps.

"You go back and pay your respects to Reverend and his wife," she'd command. It didn't matter if they were next door or a mile back up the road; I obeyed. But silently, I built up a mighty resentment. I loved Muh'Dear, but something inside of me hated her too.

Mad as I might have been over whuppings, punishments, or Muh'Dear telling me how I was no different, I looked around every night at the dinner table and still knew I was safe.

"There's nothin' more in this world than havin' your family around you, Meechee," Muh'Dear always preached. Like most of what she said, it went in one ear and out the other, at least that's what I thought at the time.

The days started early with the smell of Granddaddy's biscuits, bacon, eggs, and grits. Granddaddy didn't say much, but he believed in making his family their breakfast before he went to work at the chemical plant. I rolled out of one of the two twin beds in the room I shared with my aunties Avea and Daisy. Then I had to race my uncles Roy and Junior in order to get to the kitchen table first—just so long as Muh'Dear didn't catch us running in her house.

In L.A., at mealtime, everybody did their own thing. Muh'Dear's rules weren't like that. Out here, if you weren't at that breakfast table by 6:45, you didn't eat. Might as well have been locks on the cabinets and the icebox by 7:00.

That was just one example of how Muh'Dear ran a tight ship. One morning I sat down for breakfast and my cousin Michael reached over and took a biscuit right off my plate. I looked over at Muh'Dear to see what she'd do but her eyes were nine other places at once. I looked at Michael, who was smiling at me with a look that said "You're in the big house now."

"Don't take anything off my plate again," I told him.

But he did the same thing the next morning. There was plenty of food on the table—he did what he did because he wanted to. Muh'Dear might have said there was no disrespect out here, but Michael was disrespecting me.

So I stuck my fork in his hand.

Michael hollered.

Muh'Dear looked up.

"Both of you. Out back. *NOW.*"

The whole room went silent.

On the way out, I was sure I was about to get a whupping but as soon as we were in the backyard, Muh'Dear laid down the rules:

"No bitin', no stratchin'. Now work it out."

"No girl from California's gonna whup me." Michael was tough. He was ten and I was still eight, but I wasn't about to back down.

Looking back, I couldn't say fighting was the answer. I couldn't even say where the idea to throw the first punch came from. But when I threw it dead to his jaw, something inside just took over. I hit Michael and he hit the ground. Before he could get up, I had my knees in his chest and my fists all over his face. The whole thing took me less than ten seconds.

When it was over, Muh'Dear broke it up and whupped us both so bad we couldn't sit down for two days. But I was so proud of myself for beating a boy, I felt ten feet tall, whupping or not. Just like that, I got a reputation for being nothing to mess with. It was just one of many times that got me used to fighting and Muh'Dear's switches and belts. And the whuppings only made me more defiant.

Something else happened that summer that made the rules of Muh'Dear's house come to life. It was during a family barbecue. Tynia came around with her brother Greg. Everything was going fine, until I noticed my cousin Michael and Greg were arguing. By the time I got over there, Michael was drawing his arm back to hit Greg. I grabbed Michael's arm. It allowed Greg to swing and hit Michael. Suddenly Uncle Roy pushed past me, knocked Greg down, and started beating him like he stole something.

Then I heard Muh'Dear's voice behind me:

"Stop it!"

Roy stopped midswing.

"Let him up."

Again, Roy did as he was told.

"What happened?"

"Michael was about to hit Greg—" I blurted out.

"SPEAK WHEN YOU'RE SPOKEN TO, CHILD," Muh'Dear said with a look that let me know she wasn't playing. Then she turned back to Roy.

"Now, what happened?"

Roy said, "He hit Michael!"

"You come to *MY* house and put your hands on *MY* kin?"

"I'm sorry, Muh'Dear!!" Greg pleaded, then he apologized to Michael and Roy.

Soon as it was over, Muh'Dear pulled me aside. "Don't you ever speak out against family, Meechee." She looked me in my eyes and said, "Friends come and go but your family is forever. You don't go against your family, no matter what."

GOD, BOYS, AND GAME

Church.

Father, Son, and the Holy Spirit. John 3:16. That's all I knew about God in 1972. I liked going to church because it meant getting out of Muh'Dear's house, but I didn't know what else I was doing there.

Sitting in church, I was starting to notice boys. Some were my age; some were older. Some were thin; others were chubby. Some were light skinned, some were dark skinned. Some boys paid attention in church and other boys didn't, like Johnny and James Drummond. When Reverend would preach and the choir praised God, Johnny and James would be looking at me. Why was it making me feel funny?

It was a new feeling I didn't understand, especially since all the boys I knew were silly. But Johnny and James were different. They put butterflies in my stomach every time I caught them looking. Maybe I just liked the attention. Whatever it was, I couldn't figure it out. Then one Sunday I was walking out of church when those two brothers came at me at the same time.

"Who gets to have you?" James asked me.

"Huh?" I asked back. "What you talking about?"

"Which one of us is gonna be your boyfriend?" Johnny said.

Boyfriend?

Which one "gets" me?

Before I could talk back, Johnny swung on James and those two were fighting over me. I liked the attention but what they said made me confused and angry. What did they think I was, a doll or something? Nobody *owned* me. Still, something was exciting about it.

"That's the Game, girl," my auntie Anne told me. "You just had your first taste." Anne was nineteen and fine. Auntie turned heads with a switch in her step and she knew it.

"Gimme some money." She'd walk right up to any man she wanted and say those words with a sexy sneer. Whoever he was, they would give it to her like it was nothing. Auntie could cast a spell on a man like nothing I'd ever seen and I wanted to be just like her.

A few days later, I was over at Auntie Anne's house. A young hustler came by named Fred. Fred must have been about twenty and he looked like a prince: tall, hair in long plaits, light-skinned, and slim. He didn't stare hard like Johnny and James, he smiled smooth and sweet.

More than Fred's height, hair, skin, and smile, something about him told me this dude wasn't a chump. Most of all, Anne didn't try to put anything over on Fred, and I hadn't ever seen her treat anyone like that.

"Is he your boyfriend?" I asked.

"No," she told me.

"Then I want him to be *my* boyfriend," I told her.

Auntie Anne laughed like she didn't believe me, but my mind was made up.

A week later, I saw Fred again. I went right up, looked him dead in the eye, and told him, "You're gonna be my boyfriend."

"You're too young," he said, bringing the butterflies back to my tummy with his smile.

"Well, I'm going to grow up," I said. "And you're going to be my boyfriend when I do." If it took me my whole life to get him, then so be it.

As it turned out, it only took a few years. By the beginning of the ninth grade, my body was developed and I wasn't a little girl anymore.

"You remember me? I'm Anne's niece."

That was what I told Fred on a warm fall night at a football game.

"I'm grown," I said. "You gonna be my boyfriend now?"

"Yeah," he said.

One word. "Yeah." It sounded all slow and thick as it flowed out over his bright white smile. One word was all he had to say.

"You know who Fred is?" my best friend, Tynia, said the next day, like I'd hit the lottery. "He's the weed man."

I didn't care about weed. I tried it and didn't like it. I cared about Fred. Whether he sold weed or not, Fred had style.

But what did I have?

Back then, I called it "goods."

"Don't give it away for free," Auntie Anne said. "It's the only gold you got. That's the Game, girl."

Lesson learned. I knew that when Tynia let her man have her goods, she got nothing back. I held out on Fred and got everything I wanted from him. Fred let me drive his new Buick Riviera, gave me money, and treated me like a queen. But for as much as Anne told me not to fall in love, I was falling for Fred.

Easter Sunday 1977. It was an ordinary holiday at Muh'Dear's house: Sunday school, 11:00 service, Easter egg hunt at church, dinner, back to church for evening service. Afterward, I asked Muh'Dear if I could go to Tynia's house but she said no, just like she always did. I couldn't tell you why, but something in me just snapped. So I left and went to Tynia's house anyway. I'd had enough of Muh'Dear's whuppings and rules and I wasn't about to go back. But I didn't know where to go next. I couldn't stay with my best friend—her house was the first place Muh'Dear would come looking for me.

An hour later, I was knocking on Fred's door.

"You can't stay here," he said. "Muh'Dear's gonna kill me if she finds out."

"Please," I begged. "I have nowhere else to go."

Fred was scared of Muh'Dear, but I wasn't turning back. I was going to stay here tonight, no matter what it took. What it took was my virginity. I gave it up and Fred forgot all about Muh'Dear.

The next morning I went back and forth to the pay phone at the corner, begging my mom to let me come home. She tried to convince me to go back to Muh'Dear, apologize, and tough out the rest of the school year, but there was no way. Two days later, the cops came. They took me home and took Fred to jail for statutory rape, but I wouldn't tell the police he touched me, so they had to let him go.

Soon as I walked through Muh'Dear's door, I knew there was going to be trouble. When I looked in her eyes, I saw the pain and shame of having her family business dragged through the street. She was angry!

"SIT DOWN AND DON'T SAY A WORD," Muh'Dear told me.

I sat down.

Muh'Dear began to speak, laying down the law. "You're goin' to the doctor," she said, "and if you're pregnant, you're havin' that baby."

I stood up out of my chair, being defiant. "But I didn't do anything!"

Muh'Dear calmly left the room.

Where was she going? I thought. My question was answered when I saw Muh'Dear coming through the house with a double-barreled shotgun. She was through talking!

I took off. I didn't stop running until I was at Auntie Anne's house. I know I broke an Olympic record that night.

The next morning, things quieted down.

Muh'Dear forgave me after I apologized.

And the day after school was over, I went straight back to California.

GOING BACK TO CALI

I was coming home from the airport in Mom's new Lincoln MKV, stopped at the corner of Rodeo and La Cienega when it hit me—I wasn't in the country anymore.

In the next lane over was a fully loaded canary yellow Cadillac with yellow leather interior. The driver was dressed in a hat and suit to match the car. His radio was tuned to KDAY and they were blasting "Brick House" by the Commodores. As the light turned green, the man behind the wheel gave me a nod as he turned the corner.

Once again, I was in another world. Everything in Los Angeles moved faster than in Hattiesburg and I loved it. Mom was living near Washington and La Cienega, was pregnant, and married to a man named Arthur. Arthur was nice to me and my brothers and treated Mom like a queen. I was happy to be back with my brothers, Tony and Johnny. They took me around, I could stay out as late as I wanted, and there wasn't anyone telling me what to do or who to talk to.

Tony had grown up. He was nicely built, light complexion, and good looking. He had style. Not only that, he could talk his way into and out of just about anything. When Tony wanted a white three-piece-suit, just like John Travolta had in *Saturday Night Fever*, he asked Mom for the cash to buy it. When she said no, he smooth talked her until she gave in.

Johnny was two years younger than Tony. He was tall, chocolate, and handsome. Not as fashionable as Tony, but also nicely built. Earlier that year, Johnny got jumped by some gang members and they took his leather jacket. When he got home, he got another whupping for coming home without it.

By the time I got home from Mississippi, Johnny was rough and tough and nothing to mess with. When he had a beef, he let his fists do the talking.

Still, Johnny got what he wanted from Mom too. Instead of a John Travolta suit, Johnny wanted karate lessons. Instead of smooth talking her, he just kept asking until she gave in.

There was a double standard for my brothers and me. When I asked for things I wanted, Mom said no and that was the end of it. Begging didn't work for me; Muh'Dear had broken me up from begging a long time ago.

One night, Johnny and his friends went downtown to see Bruce Lee's *Enter the Dragon* and brought me along. I was mesmerized. This little Chinese dude was tough like Johnny, yet cool like Tony—he could whup you, outfox you, or both.

I had a good time with my brothers. But when I tried to brush my teeth that night, the water had been turned off.

The next afternoon, I was across the street at my friend Dana's house when the Helms doughnut truck hit the block, honking that horn that brought everybody running. As the doughnut truck pulled over, a maroon Cadillac pulled up behind him. When the driver got out, he was sharply dressed to match the car. When I looked at him, he looked familiar. It came to me that he was the same guy from the corner of Rodeo and La Cienega. I thought, *How many Cadillacs and suits does this guy have?*

"Gimme an old-fashioned buttermilk and whatever these kids want," he said, waving at the children already swarming the truck. I watched as he pulled a knot of twenties out of his pocket with a rubber band around it, peeled a bill off the top, and told the doughnut man, "Keep the change."

I got a twister and a milk and said, "Thank you, sir," then added, "Did you know it was my birthday?"

He stopped, slowly turned around, lowered his glasses, and looked me dead in the eye. He knew I was hustling him. And I knew he knew. But I didn't look away. After a second, he smiled, went in his other pocket, pulled out another knot—this one was hundreds—peeled one off, and handed it to me.

"Happy birthday." He nodded and strolled off.

DAFF

I WANTED A BOYFRIEND.

I wanted another Fred. I wanted someone easy on the eyes who had money. But the guys in my neighborhood were knuckleheads.

July 4th. Out on the sidewalk, the local guys were shooting craps. I couldn't hear the TV for all the noise they made, so I went out on the balcony to see what was going on.

An hour later, a clean Buick Regal pulled up. The guy who stepped out was tall, dark, and nicely dressed, and if the boys at the curb were loud before he showed up, they got louder as soon as he joined the game.

Who was that?

I didn't know much about gambling. When I heard my mom say the word, it was a problem. Arthur had a gambling problem. My real dad had a gambling problem. Tony had a gambling problem. Nobody who gambled ever seemed to get ahead. But looking at that dice game down on the street, I know what I saw: When this guy started shooting, he won. When it looked like he had the game cleaned out, he started fronting people money to keep the game going. And by the time the sun went down, he'd cleaned the game out all over again.

What I saw about him, though, interested me more: he never once got hotheaded or violent. He was always smiling. He was always the center of attention and everybody loved him.

As the neighborhood kids came out and started lighting firecrackers, the guy in the Buick gave everybody their props and drove away. Tony came up the stairs, broke but smiling.

"Who's that guy in the Buick?" I asked.

"Daff," Tony said.

"What's he do?" I asked.

"Besides take everybody's money?" He laughed. "He sells weed."

Suddenly, I started noticing Anthony "Daff" Mosley everywhere. Any time there was a dice game going on my block, sooner or later Daff would show up with a beautiful smile and a patient hustle nobody saw but me. There was a sweetness to this dude I couldn't deny. People wanted to be near him because he was so mellow and because he handed out cash like a street philanthropist. He wasn't rude, mean, or cocky, and his money and fame didn't go to his head.

I got more curious the next time I ran into my girl Sonya.

"Daff took me to the Michael Jackson concert," she said. "We were so close to the stage, I could see the sweat on his face."

"What was he like?" I asked.

"Oh my God! Amazing!" she said. "He sang 'Off the Wall' and 'ABC' and—"

"Daff," I said. "Was he all up in your business for some play or what?"

"Not really," Sonya said, sounding a little disappointed. "He didn't try anything."

Waitaminute—I already knew this guy was a hustler. And he paid all that money for front-row seats to the hottest show in town and didn't try to get anything for it?

Now I was curious and started giving Sonya the third degree.

"What was he wearing?"

"Tailored slacks and a fine silk shirt."

"How did his hair look?"

"Good."

"Did his breath smell?"

"No!"

"What about his nails?"

"Manicured."

"Did he open the car door for you?"

"Yes."

"How did he talk?"

"He was polite."

"Did he cuss?"

"Not at all."

"Was he funny? Did he make you laugh?"

"I guess..."

"Did he talk to any other girls at the show?"

"No, he just paid attention to me."

"Were you feeling him?" I asked.

"Maybe a little." She shrugged. "He's a *nice* guy."

"You don't want Daff," I finally said. "Let me have him."

A couple weeks later, the summer was over. Me and my friend Anita were walking home from school when Daff pulled up on us in his '63 Impala convertible and laid it right in the middle of the street. Soon as he lowered the hydraulics on that car, I almost lost my mind. I was done.

"You girls want a ride?" he asked, looking right at me with that big, beautiful smile.

When we dropped Anita at her house, Daff asked, "You want to get something to eat? Maybe hit the mall after?"

"Sure," I said, and smiled back at him.

I'm feeling him... I hope he's feeling me.

"What you wanna be when you grow up?" Daff asked me over dinner. By now, he had brought me to Marie Callender's, which was way better than the best place I knew—McDonald's. I still couldn't get over that the menu was in my hands and not on the wall.

"I'm gonna be a track star," I told him. "I'm going to win the gold medal in the two-twenty and the hundred in the Olympics. My coach said so." I told him about my family and he told me about his. Daff's mom owned a house over on Carlin and Hauser, which impressed me.

Eventually I had to use the ladies' room and excused myself. On my way, I heard our waiter tell the manager the old couple at the booth next to us didn't have enough money to pay for their meal. On my way back, I paused to watch Daff slip the waiter a fifty, pointing at the old folks' table. He didn't make it a big deal, even after the old couple came by to say thank-you. He just said, "Yes ma'am," and "No, ma'am," to them, just like I would have.

Sonya wasn't lying. This guy WAS nice.

"What do *you* wanna be when you get older?" I asked Daff, later at the Fox Hills Mall.

"Paid," he answered. "Maybe own a club."

As we walked through the mall, I looked at the stores and realized I didn't know a thing about style—I didn't even know what a name brand was. With Mom, everything I owned came off the sale rack at Zody's and White Front. It was on the tip of my tongue to lie about it being my birthday, but Daff spoke first.

"Get whatever you want."

"What, like an outfit?"

"Anything. Get anything you want."

I didn't get it at first…

…But I caught on fast.

For the next three hours, we hit all the stores: the Show-Off, the Casual Corner, Miller's Outpost, Foot Locker, and the Broadway, just to name a few. He waited patiently while I tried on everything I wanted and when I was done, he paid. We didn't stop until the mall closed.

This was WAY better than my birthday.

On the way home, I asked him, "Why do they call you Daff?"

"When I was a kid, they called me Daffy," he told me.

"You mean like Daffy Duck?" I said.

"Yeah."

"Kids used to call me Olive Oyl," I told him. "It bothered me. But nobody calls me that now."

"Put a stop to it, huh?" he asked.

"Yep," I said, and left it at that.

"I'm thinking you're not the one to mess with," he joked.

I laughed and told him I wasn't really that tough,

but as I said it, something stirred inside. I hadn't even *thought* about being called Olive Oyl in years. *Why was I opening up to this guy?* I let it drop, but I was feeling something. And it wasn't just his money.

By the time I got home, it was late. When we pulled up in front of my Mom's place, Daff slid a little Zales box across the seat. Inside was a pair of diamond earrings.

I was in shock. With Fred, it was about candy and soda and driving his car but this—this whole afternoon—was on an entirely different level. I'd never imagined having diamonds of my own. The clothes were one thing...I had clothes. *But diamonds?* The closest I'd come to jewelry was trying on Mom's rings as a little girl. And here was this man buying me diamonds!

"Think I could see you tomorrow?" Daff asked.

"Yeah, I guess." Like I was really going to say no. Far as I was concerned, he could take me out whenever he wanted.

After that first date—at least in my mind—Daff was my boyfriend.

CONTROL

Looking back over my high school years:

I had a man—Daff.

I wore all the latest fashions from head to toe; if it was fly, I had it.

Star of the track team—that was me.

Most popular at Hamilton High School—yours truly.

And on top of that, if you needed some weed, I had that too.

I had everything under control.

By the end of the eleventh grade, I got what I wanted. God forgive you if you crossed me because I wouldn't.

Me, confused? No way.

I had it all figured out.

I was in charge.

I was in control.

I knew I was especially in control at the big year-end track meet against Crenshaw High, Hamilton's archrivals. The winner was going to the city finals, then state, then all-American. If I was going to get scholarship money and go to the Olympics like I'd told Daff, these races were must wins. I was the reason we were favored. Our coach, Miss Jones, might have been calling the shots, but I was running the show: high-stepping across the finish line, trash-talking our competition, sometimes even trash-talking my own teammates.

"Pace yourselves today," Miss Jones preached. "We know we can win this one, so don't get cocky." She looked right at me when she said it.

Strike one.

Then she had the nerve to take me aside and say, "No showboating today. Just run your races clean."

Now this woman was telling me how to handle my business?

Strike two.

"And remember," she pushed when I gave her a look, "this is not your team, it's *my* team."

Strike three.

Nobody talked to me like that.

Just before the 440, I went and huddled up my girls. "We're losing."

"We can't lose," somebody said. "This is Crenshaw High. This is the finals. This is what we worked for all year—"

"I don't care about Crenshaw High and I don't care about the finals. We. Are. Losing. This. Race."

I didn't care about my team any more than I cared about that race. I cared about me, and I was going to send a message to Miss Jones, my teammates, everybody at school, and everybody I knew: I was in control.

Soon as the starter pistol went off, my first-leg runner took a quick lead.

Second-leg held on.

I stared daggers at both girls and moved 'em off my good side.

Third-leg was my girl Felicia. She saw me looking back at her from my starting position and my eyes said it all...

...Don't you even THINK about crossing me.

As Felicia took the baton, the entire stadium started to buzz. Felicia was slowing down, the Crenshaw girls were catching up. By the time I got the baton, the entire place was silent. So silent, you could hear the bells in my braids as I jogged: *shing-shing-shing-shing.*

Nobody could believe what they were seeing, not even the Crenshaw girls.

But they knew.

Everybody knew.

This was my race.

And I could do what I wanted.

As I crossed the line in dead last, ending our season and throwing everything we'd worked for down the drain, I stared right at Miss Jones and now *she* knew: I was in control.

I was running high on my power. But running races was one thing. Running the street was something else.

All year long, Daff had been sponsoring me. Ever since our first date, I'd been holding out on him even harder than I had with Fred. I'd give him a little play to keep him happy, but the rest of me was always just out of reach. I wasn't the only girl in town, though.

There were a lot of girls after Daff, like Gigi Jackson. My girl Felicia overheard her in history class saying how she was going to take Daff from me.

What??

Nobody was taking my man!!

The next Saturday, Daff and I were together, riding to the Burger King on Crenshaw where everybody hung out, top down, radio blasting GQ's "I Do Love You."

When we pulled up, who do I see—Gigi. I don't even remember opening the door. The next thing I know, Daff was pulling me off of her.

What just happened?

"What did I do?" I asked Daff on the way home. I honestly couldn't remember.

Daff told me, "Before I could park, you jumped out the car and were beating on that girl like you were trying to kill her. Talking about, 'ain't nobody takin' your man.'" Then he added, "Did I miss something?"

It was like I saw red. I realized that when it came

to Daff, I had no control. When I looked in his eyes, I think Daff realized it too. But there was something else. Anne used to tell me, "Don't fall in love."

But I had.

And things were about to get a lot more complicated.

TURNED OUT

All the time I'd been holding out on Daff didn't mean I wasn't having sex. In fact, the sex I was having put me up even higher in my little mind. I was feeling Daff, but I was also feeling a thug on my block, Lonzo.

Lonzo was the opposite of Daff in every way. He was short, muscular, sneaky looking, and had a mean glint in his eye. Instead of sweat suits and tailored slacks, Lonzo wore a golf hat, Dickies, Locs, and a blue Pendleton that identified him as a Westside Crip. And while his demeanor ran most folks off, it attracted me.

Shortly after the Burger King incident, I was out on Dana's front porch one afternoon, braiding her hair. Lonzo was standing on the balcony next door when two doors down, a dude named Bee, who owed Lonzo money, stepped out to the ice cream truck as it came down the block.

One minute, Lonzo was staring at me with that

smile. The next thing I knew, he was over the second-story railing. Soon as he hit the ground, he ran at Bee and hit him so hard everyone on the block could hear it. Before Bee hit the ground, Lonzo ripped the pocket off Bee's pants in order to collect his debt.

No way Daff would do that.

There it was—that killer instinct. I wondered if Lonzo felt what I felt right before I beat Gigi down. I wonder if he saw red too. My brothers and girl friends all said:

"Girl, that boy ain't about nothin'."

"He dogged out every girl he's ever been with."

"Lonzo is bad news."

But I didn't care—the more reckless he was, the more I wanted him. Except Lonzo had no money and I didn't understand why. He had a job at the Datsun dealership and was a shot caller on the street. So how come he was still broke? I knew he smoked sherm—cigarettes dipped in PCP—but his get-high wasn't where all his money went. Something didn't add up.

Didn't matter, though. I was getting money from Daff, and I could still mess with Lonzo on the down-low. Once again, I was on top of the world. All my girls looked up to me. When either one of my men would come around, they'd go, "Ooh, look at her."

What woman doesn't like attention?

Even when I got busted, I still thought I was cool. One day, I left school to get with Lonzo. But when I came out of the cafeteria door, Lonzo was on one side of the street and Daff was waiting on the other.

I didn't think, *I'm busted.*

I thought, *How am I gonna play this?*

Lonzo looked at Daff, then looked at me and said, "Who are you going with?"

I saw the hurt in Daff's eyes but knew what I had to do and shouted, "Don't look at me like that," as I hopped in Lonzo's car. "Nobody told you to come up here."

No way was I going to break my routine, my control.

It made sense in my sick little mind. Even when I gave Lonzo my goods and he was done with me, I just picked up the phone, called Daff, smoothed it all out, and we went shopping. Looking back, I was crazy for messing over a guy like Daff and a fool for letting Lonzo dog me out. But I was having it my way.

Until I found out I was pregnant.

"How do you know it's mine?" Lonzo asked.

"You're the only guy I've been with" was all I could say.

All Lonzo said was, "Here's some money. Get an abortion."

Right then, my fantasy crumbled. Lonzo wasn't my boyfriend and I didn't mean anything to him. More importantly, our baby didn't mean anything to him.

Most of all, I was scared of what my mom was going to do. So I cut school one day, went to Kaiser, and met with a doctor.

"Are you sure?" she asked.

"Well," I answered, "pretty sure."

"You need to be sure," she told me. "And you need to have your parents' permission."

As I walked home, I realized there wasn't any easy way around it. I was sure about that abortion before. But now that I had to tell Mom, maybe I wanted to keep this baby.

"You don't have room in your life for a baby," Mom said. "What are you going to do with a baby when you're just a baby yourself? Have you told Daff yet?"

"No," I lied. I wouldn't have heard the end of it if I'd told her the truth.

"You're going to wind up giving the child to me," Mom said as my baby brother, Cliff, began to cry for his bottle. "And I have enough to handle."

I was confused and scared, and by the time my track coach showed up—my mom had called and told her what was going on—I couldn't think straight.

"Jemeker," Coach said. "The last thing you want to do is have this baby. You've got a future. You're going to Tennessee State to be a track star, just like Wilma Rudolph. You need to do this. You've got too much to lose."

"You need to do this" got me back to that hospital.

"Too much to lose" got me up onto that cold operating table.

Having that abortion hurt worse than anything I'd ever felt. And it was the scariest thing I'd ever been through. But worst of all, it brought a horrible emptiness I'd never felt before.

GET IN WHERE YOU FIT IN

I hated Lonzo for what he'd done to me and, yes, my heart was broken. But Daff was my light in a time of darkness and it took my heart being broken to let him in. Daff played along with the lie I told Mom, even though he knew the baby hadn't been his. During those dark days, Daff visited all the time, brought me food and presents, and took Mom's third degree with a laugh and a smile.

One day toward the end of the eleventh grade, my brother Johnny was on his way out the door to mess with Ethyl, Mom's neighbor downstairs. Mom didn't care for Ethyl and always told him so, but Johnny never listened—Ethyl had him sprung.

When Mom tried to block the door, Johnny snapped. By the time I knew what was going on, Mom was trying to get her hands on the butcher knife and Johnny was trying to drag her out of the kitchen. So I jumped on Johnny. After all my years with Muh'Dear, I wouldn't dream of going against my own mother. What could Mom have done to make my brother think he could put his hands on her?

Johnny went to jail behind the incident and when he got out, he moved in with Ethyl. Then Tony went to jail for arson. That left Mom, Cliff, Fernando, and myself. By then, Mom and Arthur had separated. Shortly after that, Mom got orders from the air force to be stationed in Japan for active duty for six months.

"You need to watch the baby," she told me.

She worked it out with the liquor store so that I could cash her checks and pay the bills. But I was still in school! How in the world was I supposed to take care of my infant brother? How was I supposed to have a life of my own? I couldn't have a baby of my own because I was supposed to have a future and suddenly I had to take care of my little brother? Now, it was just me and Cliff.

When I mentioned it to Daff, he said, "Don't worry. I'll help you."

Daff moved in and continued to show the quality of his character. He became the man of the house. He never complained once. And I found myself falling deeper in love with him.

That year, Daff picked me up every night at work. He bathed and fed baby Cliff. When Cliff and I caught a cold, Daff took us both to the doctor. He even got us medicine and chicken soup, just because the doctor said so.

That year, I grew up not a minute too soon. More than a couple girl friends had also gotten pregnant, except they dropped out of school and ended up on welfare.

Daff became my whole world. I knew what I had with him and it wasn't just about a paycheck. It was about something real. It was about a future. But exactly what kind of future was still uncertain. Graduation was coming up and I already had furniture on layaway. I already knew we'd be moving into our own place as soon as I turned eighteen. But I needed a plan.

Thanks to Daff, we had a lot, but I wanted more. When I started looking for opportunities to get it done, the first one was clear: toughen up my game. Daff was such a nice guy he let people slide on credit and folks took advantage. That made me upset. Here we were, trying to get ahead, and somebody was always coming around asking for free weed, gambling money, a loan, or some kind of handout.

"Why'd you do that?" I asked one day after I stood on the patio and watched him give Lonzo a free sack.

"Don't worry," he said.

But this time, I did. In my eyes, folks weren't just

taking advantage of Daff, they were taking advantage of me too. And Lonzo of all people?

Time to take control.

The next time I saw Daff handing Lonzo some weed, I was looking to make sure Lonzo handed him some money. When he didn't, I ran downstairs, grabbed the sack out of Lonzo's hand and got right in his face.

"When you can pay for it," I told him, "you can get it. That goes for everybody. Enough is enough."

Soon, everybody got the message: if Daff was going to be the nice guy, I was going to be the one who said NO so he didn't have to. Playing that role came naturally—messing with my man was the same as messing with my money. From then on, I checked everybody. I even checked Daff's mom when I found out she was charging him rent, even though he lived with me and Cliff. Nobody stood up to Daff's mom, Alice, but I did.

"Daff's not paying for a roof where he doesn't lay his head," I told her.

"Mind your own business!" she told me.

I didn't even bother answering her. Daff and weed *were* my business. And I was watching my money.

CURB SERVING

It was June 1980. Graduation day. I was excited. My family was there and so was Daff.

Mom was so happy. When I walked across the stage to receive my high school diploma, I saw the look on her face. I knew she was proud, and it made me feel good to see her so happy.

"You made it," Mom said. "Now what are you going to do?"

"Take some pictures, say good-bye to my friends, and go eat."

"Girl," she said, taking the fun out of the moment, "you know what I'm talking about."

"Mom, don't worry... I got it. This is a happy moment for me. I don't want to think about all that now."

"Enjoy your day, but we're going to talk about this," she said. "You're going to college."

After I took a few pictures and said good-bye to my

friends, we went to eat at Sizzler. I wasn't thinking about college, my business, or anything other than enjoying the moment. But I knew my mom—when she started something, she was going to finish it.

A few days later, we were eating breakfast. Cliff was still asleep and Mom had me to herself.

"So now what are you going to do?"

I knew this was coming. I went in my backpack, laid out my registration forms to LACC and East LA Community College, and showed Mom the classes I was going to take. I was going to go to school, I was going to run track, and I was going to get my money.

"You know I handle my business," I told Mom.

"Business?" she said. "You don't have any business."

If she only knew.

Mom had found a new apartment on Twelfth Avenue off Venice Boulevard. I would have moved in with Daff the day after graduation, but Mom wouldn't have it.

"Until you're eighteen," she said, "you're my responsibility. After that, you can do whatever you want."

As we were moving in to Mom's new place, I noticed a tall, skinny guy named Ricardo who stayed upstairs with his mom. Game recognized Game; it didn't take me long to see Ricardo was selling weed to all his friends, just like I was. And it didn't take me long to see an opportunity. I wanted to build my business. I wanted

Ricardo working for me. But I knew I had to come at him the right way.

"If you know anybody looking for some weed," I told him, "let me know." Once I slid him a sample to let him know what I had, it was a done deal. We were in business.

And right off the bat, business was great. Thanks to the quality of my weed, traffic got too heavy at the door and we had to take it to the curb. Where there had been nothing a month ago, now there was a full-on weed spot with customers round the clock. Every night I stood on that corner like I owned it, a skinny little girl sticking out in a bright pink Fila tennis outfit and matching shoes. But the police were more interested in the Winchell's Donut House down the street than they were in my business. What I used to sell in a week only took hours, sometimes minutes. And anyone buying or selling—whether they knew it or not—was getting their weed from me.

September 1, 1980. I was finally eighteen. Me and Daff moved into our own place off of Washington, on Fourth Avenue—a one-bedroom duplex at the end of the block. Ricardo stayed on Twelfth Avenue and handled the nickels, dimes, and twenties. And I dealt with preferred customers directly.

Christmas Eve 1980. Daff came home to a decorated

house and a romantic candlelight dinner I had prepared for him. After we ate, we opened our gifts: I got Daff sweat suits in a dozen colors and Jordache jeans in every style I could find. He got me a Louis Vuitton bag. When I opened the bag, I found a car key. When I looked out the window, there was a black-on-black Mercedes convertible 450SL.

Life is good.

PART II

COCAINE

THE COST OF DOING BUSINESS

It was the very end of 1980. I was watching *Dallas* on a Friday night.

J. R. Ewing was driving my Mercedes.

Charlene Tilton had a Louis Vuitton bag just like the one Daff gave me.

Sue-Ellen and Pamela wore Mercedes and Adrienne Vittadini clothes and so did I.

But I looked at their house and I looked at our house and the similarities ended. The Ewings lived in a mansion on a ranch. The Ewings had land, houses, businesses, oil, and cattle . . . an empire. We were hood rich. We'd got everything cash could buy but were running out of places to put it. We had cars but not enough garage space.

I wanted to live like they lived on *Dallas*.

The question was how.

A week later, Daff called me collect. "Baby, I'm locked up." I said, "Locked up? What happened, where are you?" Daff could hear the panic in my voice and told me to calm down. "I'm at the Venice police station. Contact a bails bondsman and post my bail." Our conversation was cut short by the guard. I told Daff, "I love you." He said, "I love you too." Soon as we hung up, I called my mom. I didn't know the first thing about posting a bail. Mom explained how the process worked. Then she gave me the number of a bondsman named Willie. I called and told him the situation and he called the station. When Willie called back, he told me Daff got pulled over and the police found a gun in the car.

"Do you have any collateral, a house or some property?" he asked.

"No."

"Then you need ten thousand dollars."

It was nothing to have fifty or sixty thousand dollars at the house for business expenses. But this was a first. It took me three tries to get the safe open, but eventually I got it open and took the cash to meet Willie at the Venice police station. Willie pulled up to the parking lot in a money-green Rolls-Royce. When he got out in a suit, crocodile shoes, and matching belt, he looked just like a black J.R.

I was thinking, *How many people does he bail out a day?*

And, *Does everybody give this man ten thousand dollars to get out of jail?* Which led to, *I want to work for him.*

So the next day, I picked up the phone and called him. Willie was happy I called and invited me to his house, up at the top of Baldwin Hills. I got to the house and thought, *This guy* is *J.R.! He's got the house, he's got the clothes, he's got the family... he's even got the view!*

"I want to work for you," I told him.

"Call me later in the week," he said.

He's also got J.R.'s shady smile...

When I got home, I told Daff, "This man's rich."

"A bail bondsman, Jemeker?" Daff asked. "He's a square."

"No he's not. He's got a Rolls-Royce, jewelry, a house up in the hills with a pool... he's living like the Ewings. And I want to get to know him."

Daff knew me. He knew I was going to do what I wanted. And I wanted to know everything about Willie's business. A couple days later, I met Willie for lunch. He told me what he did and how he did it.

"Was it easy for you to get ten grand together?" he asked.

"Why? You have an easier way for me to get money?"

"Maybe."

I started calling him on the regular. We met up several more times for lunch. Finally, one day, he called me.

"You ready to work?"

I told him yes. He gave me an address. I got there and it was a motel. I called him from my car phone.

"I think I'm here but it's a motel," I said.

"I'm in room 206. Come on up."

I didn't know what to expect, but I went up to the room and knocked on the door. Willie opened it and greeted me with that shady smile.

I looked around the room. It was just him. Only other thing that caught my eye was a Gucci overnight bag by the table.

Then Willie started talking my ear off: "So you really ready to work for me...hmm...you sure? You're sure you're sure? 'Cause you're not the only person I'm considering for the job...It's hard...takes concentration...better have good organizational skills...won't happen overnight, better be loyal...but if you REALLY want to make money—"

Great... now this old man talks *like J.R., too.*

"I got it," I told him, "when do I start?"

With that, he went to the overnight bag. Opened it. Pulled out a triple-beam scale. "Here's what you do: you move these weights like this and then—"

"I know what to do with one of those—" I told him, cutting him off again.

"—But do you know what to do with *this?*" he said, cutting me off right back.

I looked at what he was holding: a sandwich bag full

of cocaine. I'd never seen coke before. But if it was what got him where he was, it was what I was there for.

Made me wonder if J. R. Ewing got a sack...

He showed me how to scale the ounce into grams, halves, and quarters. Grams were a hundred. Halves were fifty. A quarter was twenty-five.

"How much you want for all this?" I asked.

"This one's on me," he said. "We'll talk about the next one...'cause I know you'll be back."

I went to the bathroom before I left. When I came out, he flipped out a roll of flavored condoms.

"What flavor you want?" he asked, smiling that smile again. I looked back and forth between Willie and the dope.

Pay to play, Jemeker, I thought. Then I started convincing myself:

You gotta take one for the team if you want to come up.

He ain't asking you to give up your goods. It's just oral.

That's how I justified it.

I picked the red one—cherry.

For the next three minutes, I went somewhere else, somewhere that wasn't worth remembering. I tried to imagine I was with Daff and not this old man, but I'd never done oral sex with him, so it was difficult. When it was done, I grabbed what I came for and got out.

Driving home, I remembered something I hadn't thought about since I was six years old.

I'm back on Sycamore Avenue. It's a warm afternoon and

I'm playing in the backyard. I look in the neighbor's house and remember I need to go check in with the old man who baby-sits me and my brothers—let him know I'm home from school.

I knock at the kitchen door and shout I'm here. He waves me in. It's dark inside, but I can see him sitting in the corner.

I go inside.

He's staring at me.

Smiling.

Waving me to come closer.

Something doesn't feel right.

He doesn't say a word.

But he unzips his fly.

Soon as I see his penis, I run home, fast as I can.

I snapped out of it just as I get home. Thank God Daff wasn't there. I went straight to the bathroom and brushed my teeth until my gums bled. Then I threw the toothbrush away. Then I gargled with Dr. Tichenor's. But I still felt dirty. And when Daff finally did make it home, I couldn't look him in the face.

But when he asked what was in the bag, I broke it down to Daff just like Willie had broken it down to me. "That bail bondsman fronted us this ounce," I told Daff, "and showed me how to work it."

"Who's gonna buy that stuff?" Daff asked.

"I don't care. Same people who buy weed."

"I don't know this old man," Daff said. Then he said something else I hadn't thought of yet: "Cocaine's the big leagues."

Daff didn't want to do it. But all I saw was money. I knew this was what I needed to take my business to the next level. And I knew I couldn't do this on my own. Besides, I couldn't turn back. Not now. Not after doing the math on cocaine versus marijuana money. Not after what I'd had to do to get this coke.

When he looked at me again, I was crying.

He didn't know what I had to do...

"Daff," I told him, "I love you. This is the chance of a lifetime. We gotta do this."

When I looked in my man's eyes, I saw into his heart. He saw into mine. He felt my pain even if he didn't understand it. Besides, my man believed in me and he was down.

"Okay," he said. "Let's get rich."

THE GOOD LIFE

Now I was thinking who could help me move the cocaine.

First person who came to my mind was Daff's cousin David, who lived in the front apartment of our duplex.

"Take this and see what you can do with it," I told David as I gave him some of the coke.

Next I called my preferred weed customers.

"Come by the house, I need to holler at you."

To my surprise, nobody went home empty-handed. By the end of the night, the team was in place and I only had a few grams left. I was trying to decide who to give the rest of the coke to when someone knocked at the door. It was David. He must've just gotten off of work; he was still in his McDonald's uniform.

"I need some more," he said.

I gave him all that I had. Now I was out of cocaine.

I was so excited that everything was gone, I called Daff to see when he was coming home.

He said, "I'm winning right now but I'll be home soon."

I said, "I'm winning too. I'll see you when you get here." As I was waiting for Daff, reality kicked in: I needed some more dope. I had to call Willie.

Yuck!

I knew what I was *not* going to do.

I needed a plan.

Hmm...

Got it!

I called Willie and apologized about the late hour.

"It's never too late to call me," he said. "I'm a bail bondsman. I get up for money—you can sleep when you're dead. What's going on?"

"My husband wants to invest in my business. When can we get together?"

There was a slight pause. Willie said, "Well, I'm playing golf in the morning, but I can give you a call when I'm done."

"Okay, great. I'll see you tomorrow. Have a good evening."

Finally Daff came home. Before he could get his key in the lock, I had the door open. I hugged him, told him how much I missed him. He hugged me back.

I pulled him into the living room. As we sat down on the couch, Daff noticed stacks of money on the coffee table. I scooped up the cash and handed it to him.

As he was counting it, I told him, "Baby, that ounce went sooooo fast."

"You made all this off of one ounce?"

"Yep."

"Call the old man," Daff said. "I want to get some more."

"I already did," I told him.

The next morning, we got a call from Willie. An hour later, he pulled in the driveway. Willie and Daff hit it off from the start. Willie was gracious and friendly to Daff, playing it up like we were doing him a favor, selling his drugs for him. Daff was Daff—reading the situation, playing his position, making Willie feel like the man.

I watched them both: knowing what I knew, it was a win-win situation. To Willie, Daff represented connections so he didn't have to get his hands dirty. To Daff, Willie was the plug to the drugs. Willie needed Daff. Daff needed Willie. And I was right in the middle, the glue holding this thing together.

In less than a month, Willie was bringing us a key at a time.

One key turned to two.

Two turned to four.

Business blew up. If I wasn't collecting the money, I was counting it: hundreds went into the safety deposit box because they took up less room. We used fifties and twenties to buy more dope; they were easier to count. When we were done counting, we drove up to our safety deposit box on Wilshire and Beverly Drive. Nine to five, Monday through Friday, the cocaine business was our full-time job.

But on my weekends, I shopped.

I went to Beverly Hills. I brought Anita and Sonya with me. We hit Fila, Ellesse, Gucci, Chanel, Giorgio, and Lina Lee. "You see something you want, get it," I told my girls. I did the same. After our shopping spree, we celebrated at the Black Whale in Marina Del Rey with lobster and steak.

Daff also elevated his lifestyle. He hired my dad to remodel his mom's whole house, then filled it with brand-new furniture. Then he had Dad turn the garage into a laid-out gambling shack: wood walls, crap table, hi-fi stereo, Italian leather couch, big-screen TV, and satellite dish. He and his boys also went to Vegas. And they didn't just drive out, they chartered a private jet.

Even with his success, Daff never forgot where he came from. He bundled up all the one-dollar bills we made into fifty-dollar stacks and gave them away throughout the neighborhood. He was especially good to the homeless; instead of giving them change, he gave them stacks.

Daff also hosted a Sunday barbecue at Cheviot Hills Park and provided the food, beverages, and music. He hired a DJ to play all the latest tunes, mixing in our favorite R&B hits with oldies.

One particular afternoon, we pulled up and I noticed two guys getting out of a convertible, custom-painted Blazer. I asked Daff if he knew them.

"Yes," he said. "And you know them too; that's Doug and Champ."

"Oh," I replied. "From the east side."

Like all the barbecues, this one had a great turnout. People were here from all around town.

We made our grand entrance. We were wearing matching outfits—Daff was in his navy blue Fila outfit, I was in my matching Fila tennis skirt.

I could feel the excitement; the barbecue was a hustler's holiday and one more way Daff took care of the people who took care of him.

He was the king.

I was his queen.

And life was good.

One day, Daff was watching the football game and saw an ad for the latest model big-screen TV. I noticed his reaction and decided to surprise him. The next morning, I went to Santa Monica to find the TV. When I walked through the door of the electronics store, I asked the guys behind the counter if they had what I was looking for. They did. I asked them what kind of deal I could get if I bought two. I negotiated a great price, paid in cash, and arranged to have them delivered.

The next day, one of the salesmen called me up to ask if everything was okay. Then he told me he had some other items I might be interested in. We set a location and a couple days later, I had a new cocaine hookup with a better price.

November 1981. I realized it had been a couple months since my last period. Daff took me to Cedars-Sinai hospital. An hour later my doctor said, "You're two months' pregnant."

When we walked out of that doctor's office, you never saw two people smile so big.

"I hope it's a girl," Daff said. "She'll look just like you."

I just hoped the baby would be healthy and that it was a boy. That way he would look just like Daff.

Soon as we got home, Daff put me on maternity leave. He didn't want me handling any of the dope, but I was still allowed to count and drop off money.

Before the baby came, Muh'Dear flew out. I needed the strongest people in my life to help me through this and no one was stronger than my grandmother. On July 27, 1982, my water broke. At first I felt no pain; within an hour I felt the most excruciating pain I'd ever experienced.

It lasted one to two minutes. After that, all I wanted was my baby out of me. That didn't happen! I was in labor twenty-three hours and fifty-one minutes. At 4:06 a.m. I gave birth. I was exhausted.

But when I saw my beautiful baby boy it was all worth it.

He looked just like his daddy.

There were no words to express the joy I felt.

THE BEST AND THE WORST

A few months after Anthony was born, we drove to Las Vegas in Daff's Cadillac. Every day for the past few years, we'd devoted ourselves to family, friends, and business associates. Now it was time to do something for us.

We got a suite at Caesars Palace, then went to the wedding chapel across the street from Circus Circus.

Time to make it official.

Daff was nervous, but as we took our vows I saw my dreams become reality. Having my baby and marrying the man I loved were priceless.

When we got back to L.A., we moved into a spacious four-bedroom house on Fifty-fourth Street. Not only did it have a big backyard, but it was next to a park—perfect for when Anthony got a little older.

But just when we'd settled in and everything seemed all right, the phone rang.

As Daff listened on the other end, I knew something was wrong. He had an expression on his face that I'd never seen before.

"Baby," I asked. "What is it?"

"Glen got shot," he replied. "He's dead."

I was in disbelief! Glen worked for us, he had just left our house. When I thought about his wife and the children being fatherless, I thought about our family without Daff. I was overcome with emotion. My emotions were interrupted by the doorbell; it was my brother Johnny. He had heard what happened and came over to check on us. I told him, "I don't know what's going on or why somebody would shoot Glen, but I do know I want you with my husband at all times."

Our condolences went out to Glen's family. When services were held the following week, Daff and I covered the charges. We also gave his wife and children money every month to help with the bills. We did everything we could. Glen's death was devastating to everyone. It was the first time anything like this had happened to one of our workers.

A few weeks later, Daff and I were having breakfast at M & M, a little place on West Boulevard that was always packed with people we knew. So it wasn't surprising when Chris, another one of our workers, spotted us and ran over.

"Hey, Daff," he said eagerly. "The guy I was telling you about is here and he wants to meet you. Can I bring him over?"

"What do you think, babe?" Daff asked me.

"Who is he?" I asked Chris. I didn't trust anyone we didn't know.

"Don't worry," Chris replied, "he's cool. And he's making money."

"Go on and get the dude so I can finish my breakfast," Daff told him.

Chris came back with a fat, dark-skinned guy wearing Cazal glasses, nugget jewelry, and Gucci tennis shoes.

"Daff, this is Juda."

"I've heard a lot of good things about you," Juda said, shaking Daff's hand but looking at me. "Here's my number. Give me a call when we can link up."

"All right," Daff replied. "Nice meeting you."

When Juda left, I handed Daff a Wet-Nap. "Wipe your hands off. There's no telling where his hands have been."

Daff took one look at me and smiled.

"You don't like him, huh?"

"Not particularly," I responded. "Plus, I don't know him."

That was the difference between my husband and me. Where I saw a problem, Daff saw opportunities.

Not long after that, we went to dinner with Juda, not once but twice. As far as I was concerned, once was too much. Not only was he rude and disrespectful, but he brought a different woman each time and introduced each of them as his wife.

I was against it, but Daff and Juda went into business together. It wasn't long before Daff started coming home later and later. When I would ask, he always told me he'd been out with Juda.

We used to be together every day. If we weren't together, we were talking on the phone. Now I had to call him on his SkyPager and wait for him to call me back.

Me, waiting?

What part of the Game was that?

I never waited for anything!

One night, I paged Daff and he didn't call me back at all. When the phone finally rang, it was Juda. I hadn't expected to hear his voice—he never called the house—and to make matters worse, he said he was looking for Daff.

Daff was supposed to be with Juda!

"He's not here," I said, and hung up the phone.

Where was my husband?

I needed some answers. So I went out to one of Daff's other cars. When I searched it, I found a bunch of unpaid parking tickets.

Now why does he have all of these? I thought. *And where did he get 'em?*

I noticed the tickets had consecutive dates and times and they were all written on the same street. It was starting to make sense. I was getting answers to my questions, even though the truth hurt.

But what hurt me was going to kill him.

I went back inside and boiled some water for a hot cup of tea. After adding some honey, lemon, and mint leaves for flavor, I sat down at the dining room table and sipped my tea. I could only guess what he was really doing, and the later it got, the more my imagination took me places I didn't want to go.

At 3:00 a.m., I heard a key turn in the lock. I picked up my gun. When the door opened, I started firing.

Daff dodged the bullets, ran to his car, and drove off. When he called a few minutes later, he yelled, "Are you crazy?! I can't believe you're shooting at me!!"

"And I can't believe you're cheating on *ME*!" I replied. "I'm telling you right now: no woman's getting you or any of the money I worked hard for—believe that!!"

"Girl, I'm not cheating on you and I can't deal with this right now," he said. "I'm tired and I'm going to sleep at my mother's house. We'll talk about this later." Then he hung up.

I couldn't believe he had just hung up the phone on me! We were in the middle of a conversation!

Uh-uh.

I knew my husband better than he knew himself.

This was more serious than I thought and I had to get to the bottom of it. I picked up the phone, dialed *Find It 411,* and gave them the address off one of the tickets. They gave me the location and the cross streets. Then I put on my tennis shoes, tied my hair up, grabbed my car keys, and dropped Anthony off at my mom's.

When I found the street, I saw the address was an apartment. I pulled around to the alley behind the building and couldn't believe what I saw...

...Daff's truck.

When I saw the truck, it felt like an elephant was standing on my chest. I pulled over to the side and opened the door. By the time I was out of my car, the pain had turned to anger. I picked up a Schlitz Malt Liquor bottle off the ground and slung it at the windshield of the truck, like Bob Gibson throwing a fastball. As the window shattered, the car alarm was deafening.

A moment later, some strange chick ran out to the truck in nothing but a robe. When I saw her cut the alarm off, I knew she had Daff's keys.

This was even better than him coming out.

Now I know who she is and I'm-a let her know who I am...

Miss Home Wrecker was so busy trying to take care of my man's truck, she didn't see me coming. I grabbed her hair with one hand and beat her with the other one.

Just when the introduction was getting good, I heard gunfire.

Uh-oh.

Time to go.

As I was running to my car, I looked up and saw Daff. He wasn't wearing a shirt, and he was carrying a big gun.

I didn't wait around to see if I could dodge his bullets.

When I got home the sun was coming up. I reloaded my gun. Then I called my father and asked if he could come change the locks to the house.

"Is everything okay?" Dad asked.

"Everything's fine. Daff lost his keys and I just want to be on the safe side."

"All right, baby. I'll see you soon."

As soon as I hung up with Dad, Mom called.

"Oh," she said, "you finally decided to answer that thing."

"Sorry, Mom. I left my cell phone at home and just got back. Do you want me to come pick up my son?"

"No, he's still sleeping. He's fine over here."

My dad arrived and installed the locks in no time. I thanked him and tried to pay him but he wouldn't accept any money.

I went inside and ran a warm bubble bath. As the

water ran, my pager kept going off. It was Daff. I was still in no mood to talk. After my bath, I was so exhausted I was asleep before my head hit the pillow. When I woke up, the sun was going down.

WOW! How long had I been asleep?

I jumped up, got dressed, and went to pick up my son.

When I pulled up to my mother's, Daff was already there.

Great.

I don't even want to see his face.

I wonder what he told my mother?

As I got out of the car, he approached and said, "We need to talk."

"Hmm, that's funny," I replied as I walked around him. "I wanted to talk last night."

I went inside. As soon as I was through the screen door, I heard my baby's voice.

"Mommy! Mommy!"

He ran into my arms and told me he loved me. For all the drama of the day, it felt good to have my baby back in my arms. My mother said she had already fed Anthony. I thanked her and told her I'd call her later. When I opened the door, Daff was still outside.

"Where are you going?" he asked.

"Don't worry about it," I told him. "Go back to your mother's house. Anthony and I will be fine. *Trust me.* 'Cause I sure can't trust you!"

"I'm *sorry,* okay?"

"You *ARE* sorry!" I shouted. "A sorry excuse for a husband! How could you do this to me and our son?!"

He tried to speak but I cut him off. "Not here! I don't want to make a scene at my mother's house!"

"Well, where can we go?" he asked.

"You know where you can go," I told him as I drove off.

Daff called all night, but I didn't answer the phone. When he tried to come by, his keys wouldn't fit. For days on end, he called and called. Sometimes I'd talk to him, sometimes I wouldn't. Finally, he admitted to everything he'd done. He even told me that Juda had introduced him to Miss Home Wrecker.

One day my father came by. He said he wanted to spend some time with Anthony and me. He wanted us to ride with him to the San Fernando Valley so we could see the house he'd been working on.

We drove up the 405 freeway and got off on Balboa in Encino, a gorgeous neighborhood full of million-dollar homes.

My dad said, "A lot of celebrities live in this neighborhood." When we got to a particularly beautiful gated property, Dad told me, "Marlon Jackson lives up the street." Then he pushed a remote on his sun visor and the gate opened automatically. At the top of the circular driveway was an extravagant house.

"C'mon," Dad said, opening the car door for Anthony and me. "Let me show you the inside."

The house had large double doors made of maple. The foyer had marble floors, mirrored walls, and a crystal chandelier. You stepped down to the living room, which was tastefully furnished. There was also a formal dining room. The kitchen had all the top-quality amenities. The house had five bedrooms and three and a half bathrooms. The master suite had his and hers walk-in closets, a shower, a sunken whirlpool tub, a bidet, and heated marble floors. The backyard was immaculately landscaped with a custom pool and Jacuzzi. My father pointed out the security cameras and monitors throughout the house.

"Who stays here, Dad? J. R. Ewing?"

Dad laughed. "Let me show you the garage."

As we went back around front, Dad opened the garage with the same remote he used on the gate.

Suddenly Anthony screamed, "Daddy, Daddy!!"

There, in the garage, was Daff.

As Anthony ran toward his father, Daff scooped him up into a hug. Daff walked over and handed me two sets of keys: one to the house and the other to the brand-new, fully loaded BMW 633csi in the garage behind him.

Daff looked me in the eyes and said, "I love you,

please give me another chance. I want my family back!"

Maybe I was crazy, but I was no fool. I accepted the house and the car and gave him another chance.

The next few months were wonderful. We were even closer than before. Daff's birthday was coming up and I wanted to give him a surprise birthday party he'd never forget.

First, I needed a location. I checked a few venues and the most popular was the Candy Store. It was one of the hottest clubs on Sunset Strip, so I bought it for the night. I made up a who's who of L.A. VIP guest list. If your name wasn't on it, you weren't getting in.

Then I set to making the party the most elaborate affair anyone had ever seen. The decorations were fit for a king. The catering was first-class, the cake was an extraordinary creation by Hansen's Cakes. And the entertainment was second to none.

I stunned my husband the night of the party with a special gift: a custom Clenet roadster, black with a white top and white interior.

"Happy birthday, baby," I said.

Daff was speechless.

The party was the talk of the town for months.

The following summer, my cousin Nicole gave a birthday party for her husband. I didn't feel like going but had to—she was family. I didn't want to go by myself but I knew better than to ask Daff—he didn't do clubs—besides, I had had a hard enough time getting him to his own party. So I called my friend Sumer and asked her if she wanted to go.

When we arrived at the party, Nicole greeted us at the door.

"Girl, guess who's here?"

"Who?" I asked.

"The Home Wrecker," Nicole replied.

"You want me to get her?" Sumer asked.

"No. I got this," I told Sumer as I handed her my purse.

"Don't turn my party out," Nicole said. "Just give her a pass or at least wait till she's outside."

But I didn't listen. I was going to beat on her every time I saw her.

"Remember me?" I asked, tapping her on the shoulder. From the look on her face, I didn't think she did. But it didn't matter. I knew who *she* was and as I threw the first punch I let her know who *I* was. I was Daff's wife.

I hit her in the face and she dropped to the floor. Ordinarily when I knocked somebody down, I would just stomp 'em, but this was personal. I dove on top of her and continued the beating.

Next thing I knew, someone was lifting me off of Miss Home Wrecker by my waist. I looked behind me to see Champ.

"Put me down!" I told him.

When he did, I saw Doug standing there, ringside. Doug said, "Your record is still undefeated!"

"C'mon," Champ said. "Let me walk you out before the police come."

When I got home, I told Daff what had happened. I went on to explain that I was tired of Los Angeles and all the drama. "Let's move to Texas."

"Why Texas?" Daff asked.

"My best friend Tynia moved there from Mississippi. She told me Texas was a nice place to raise a family. You and I have been talking about having another baby. We have enough money," I told him. "We could open our own business and get out of the Game."

"We'll talk about it tomorrow," Daff said.

When I woke up the next morning, November 23, 1984, Daff was still sleeping. I went to the kitchen and fixed chicken wings, eggs and grits, biscuits, and smothered potatoes—all his favorite things—and prepared him his breakfast in bed. I wanted to set the tone and assure that the conversation about Texas went my way. But when I walked into the bedroom with the tray, Daff was already fully dressed.

"I don't have time to eat," he said.

"But I fixed all your favorites so we could talk and have breakfast together."

"Baby," he said, and smiled, "whatever you want. But right now, I have to go." Then he left.

I was happy. "Whatever you want" was the only reason I let him out the door. I got right on the phone and called Tynia.

"I'm coming to Texas!"

"To visit?" she asked.

"No! To live!"

"C'mon, girl!!" Tynia screamed.

Tynia and I went on for hours, planning my new life. When we hung up, I realized that for the first time ever I wasn't thinking about money. Instead, I was thinking about a better future for my family. My thoughts were interrupted by the ring of the phone. It was Daff, and he sounded happy.

"I'm winning," he said, referring to a dice game. "I love you and I'll be home soon."

I told him I loved him too and hung up.

A couple hours later, my friend Dena called.

"I heard Daff got shot at the car wash," she said. "Is it true?"

"No, girl . . . I just talked to him."

Suddenly, my pager went off. It was my friend Bridgette. I hung up with Dena and returned the call. Bridgette said the same thing.

"I heard Daff got shot. Is he okay?"

Before I could answer, the house phone rang.

"I'll call you back," I told Bridgette, as I started to get an empty feeling in my heart.

This time, it was Daff's mother.

"Daff's been shot. Can you come to my house so we can go to the hospital together?"

"Yes," I responded. "I'm on my way."

I grabbed Anthony and put him in the car. I called my mother and told her to meet me at Daff's mom's house. I jumped in the car and sped off.

By the time I got there, the whole block was jammed with cars. My mom, dad, brothers, and all my friends had already arrived. As I was walking through the door, Juda—of all people—walked up to me.

"They shot Daff at the car wash," he said with no remorse. "He's dead."

I kept my composure for the sake of my son.

But inside, I was numb.

I never made it to the hospital. Instead, I went to the morgue. His mother had broken down completely and was in no condition to go anywhere, so I asked my brother Johnny to drive me. I was feeling every bad feeling imaginable. No one said a word. There was only a cold silence in the car.

When we got to the morgue, the bad feelings got

even worse. I had to give them my husband's name and show ID. The coroner led us down a dark hallway. My legs felt like jelly.

We were escorted into a room. There was a body bag on top of a gurney. I walked closer. A man standing next to the gurney unzipped the bag.

I looked down and it was Daff. There were splits in his skull from the gunshot wounds, but there was still enough of his face to identify the body as my husband's.

After I made the identification, the coroner handed me a Ziploc bag containing Daff's things. They still had blood on them. That night when I got home there was a feeling of emptiness in the house and my heart; I felt confused and lonely.

The night before Daff's funeral, I sat down with my son and tried to explain what was going on. "We'll be saying good-bye to Daddy in the morning," I told him.

He was excited and didn't understand.

I didn't understand either—why would someone do this to my husband? Everybody loved him.

Daff's service at the Angeles Funeral Home was enormous. People showed up in the thousands. There were police everywhere. They even had a helicopter hovering in the sky.

Inside, there was standing room only. People were

moaning and crying, trying to contain themselves. When they opened up the casket for the final viewing, Anthony cried out, "Daddy, wake up!"

Anyone who'd kept their cool up to that point lost it. There wasn't a dry eye in the place.

As I was escorted to view my husband's body for the last time, it finally hit me all at once that I would never see him again.

I passed out.

HIBERNATION

For months, I kept to myself, wearing nothing but pajamas. I was lonely, sad, and depressed. My friend Sonya moved in with us—me; my baby brother, Clifton; and Anthony—and took on all the duties of a caretaker. Sonya was an angel.

On rare occasions, I would force myself to leave the bedroom, but I couldn't escape my sadness. As I'd walk through the dining room, I thought of our last Thanksgiving together with both of our families seated around the table. I'd walk past Anthony's toy room and see Daff playing Hot Wheels with our son. When I'd go into the den and see the giant framed picture of Daff at his birthday party, standing next to his Clenet, I'd remember his surprise. The memories of how happy we were together would make me fall to my knees, curl up in a ball, and cry.

Many nights, I'd wake up, thinking I'd just heard the garage door open. I'd lay awake, waiting for Daff to come in and tell me it was all a bad dream, but he never did.

One day I heard Clifton screaming from the backyard. When I didn't hear Sonya going to see what the matter was, I looked through the sliding glass door and saw my son facedown floating in the pool.

I snatched the door open, ran outside, dived in, and pulled Anthony out. He was purple. He wasn't breathing. I performed CPR and told Clifton to call 911, but he was in shock, so I made the call, successfully pumped the water out of Anthony's lungs, and got him breathing again.

The paramedics arrived, took over, and rushed Anthony to the hospital. At the hospital, the doctors stabilized my baby and watched over him for several days to make sure he was all right.

I prayed the whole time: *Please Lord, don't take my son... I just buried my husband.*

My friends and family told me to go home. They told me to get some rest and change my clothes. But I wouldn't leave Anthony's side.

Word got out that I was at the hospital with Anthony. The day before my son was released, Reggie, one of our best workers, came by. He was very concerned about Anthony and wanted to know how I was doing. He made it clear that he was there for us and offered his help in any way possible.

"But, Jemeker," he said, "there's something I need to discuss with you."

I told him to come by the house the next day and he did just that.

"What do you want to do about business?" Reggie asked. "I'll run it for you. I'll keep everything just the way Daff had it. All you need to do is tell me when and where to pick it up. Everybody's starving. And we need some work. We have families to support…we need you."

I knew in my heart that selling drugs was wrong. I knew my business was illegal. But looking at Reggie, I realized he had kids to feed. *All* of our workers had kids to feed.

No matter how much money I had, other people were counting on me. Throughout my hibernation, I hadn't thought about work. I hadn't thought about money. I hadn't thought about business. But now I was.

"Don't worry," I told Reggie. "I'll call you tomorrow."

The next morning, I got up, took a shower, brushed my teeth, combed my hair, and cooked breakfast. Sonya came in with a look of surprise.

"You need help?" she asked.

"Nope," I replied. "But get dressed. We're going shopping."

I took some money out of the safe, stuck it in my purse, and walked out the front door. I drove straight to Nordstrom in Woodland Hills, pulled up to the valet service, and stepped out of the car.

Once we were inside, the salespeople greeted Sonya

and me with open arms, smiling and saying how much they'd missed me. They asked why I hadn't returned their messages. They asked if I had a new phone number. I told them I'd been out of town, but now I was back and ready to shop.

As they began to show me the latest sportswear, I interrupted.

"It's time for a new look," I said. "Show me what you have in business attire."

They brought out suits, heels, and business skirts, putting different ensembles together until I had an entire wardrobe matched up. Then I bought everything. What didn't fit in the car, I had delivered.

On the way home from Nordstrom, I called a stylist I knew and told him to meet us at the house. When he arrived, I showed him to Daff's closet and asked if he was interested in any of the clothes. He bought everything.

Finally, I called Willie to come over.

"I'm ready to do business again," I told him when we were face-to-face.

"How much do you want?" he asked me.

"How much do you have?" I replied.

"Quite a bit," he told me.

"I'll take it all," I told him.

Then I called Reggie. Before I could hang up the phone, he was at my house.

I told him where to pick it up.

It was back to business as usual.

IT'S ALL ABOUT THE MONEY

One day while in L.A., I visited my friend Anita, who managed an apartment building on Eighth Avenue. When I noticed there was a vacant apartment, I asked her if I could rent it.

"Of course you can," she said. "It'd be good to have you back in the neighborhood."

But I had no intentions of living there. Instead, I put one of my cousins in the place and told her she could live there rent free as long as she never had company over. I used the Eighth Avenue apartment as a drop-off for money. I never wanted my money and my drugs in the same location.

Somehow, Anita found out and confronted me.

"You're not selling drugs, are you?" she asked.

"If I am, what are you going to do about it?" I told her.

"I'm going to call the police."

"You're going to *WHAT??*" I said, and jumped on her. The only one she called was her husband to get me off of her.

We never had that discussion again.

Business was good and I was feeling a whole lot better. But whenever I would go home to my big, empty house full of memories, those familiar feelings would return.

I had to get out of that house. So I leased a condo in Encino. The day I moved in, I made a new friend, Angela. She told me her husband was a famous musician and that they were the only other blacks in the building.

One day I invited her to lunch at the Black Whale in the Marina. After we were seated, I left the table to wash my hands. On the way back, I heard someone calling my name. When I turned around, it was Juda, walking up behind me and acting like we were the best of friends. When he reached out to shake my hand, I refused it.

"I just washed my hands," I told him, "and I'm about to eat."

"Daff owed me some money," he said.

I let him know: "Any unfinished business you had with my husband, you can take it up with him. He's at the Inglewood Park Cemetery on Manchester and Prairie."

I returned to the table and noticed Angela acting

a little different. My guess was that she overheard me when I checked Juda.

For the next few weeks, Angela and I had lunch together almost every day. During our lunches, she started opening up to me about everything, even telling me she'd been cheating on her husband with a guy from Louisiana.

One day, she said, "My guy is looking for some cocaine. He usually has no problem getting it, but right now everyone is out."

She told me the price she'd been paying and asked if I knew anyone.

I didn't answer her—at least not then.

I went home that day and took a nap. When I awoke, I called Angela and told her to come by.

"I have some good news and some bad news," I said. "The good news is that I found some. The bad news is that it's more than what you've been paying. Do you still want it?"

"Girl, yes!" she said.

I got the money and she got the stuff. For months, everything was great with her paying up front. But one day, she asked me to front her.

I said I would but didn't hesitate to add, "I'll give you a week, no more. And let me make this perfectly clear: don't mess up our friendship over money!"

Angela said she'd have my money in a week. But one week turned into two and she wasn't returning my phone calls.

So I went to her house.

When she opened the door, I could see she was nervous.

"I don't know how to tell you this," she said. "The dope never made it to Louisiana and—"

I cut her off right there. "What I'm here to talk about is my money. When are you going to have it?"

"I'll have some money coming in two weeks," Angela promised. "I swear."

First she said the dope never got there, I thought, *now she's telling me she's got money coming in two weeks. She's playing with me. She's flipping my money and she's got me waiting. She may be scandalous with her men, but I'm not the one to mess with.*

I waited the two weeks and added a few days to make sure that my money was there. Then I sent my people to get it. I told them what she owed me and what I wanted. Anything more, they could have.

They had to ransack her place to find my money, but they did... and then some.

I moved out of the condo and never did business with Angela again.

BUSINESS BEFORE PLEASURE

My professional life was moving along, but my personal life was all about Anthony and family. In other words, men weren't the number one thing on my mind.

Looking back, romantic love was my blind spot. For all my business wisdom, I was not that experienced with men. I had been with Fred in Misissippi, I had been with Lonzo, and I had been with Daff, the love of my life. Players in business were one thing; players in romance were something else entirely.

Since Daff had died, I had also built up a wall that no man had scaled. But the men in my world knew I was on the market. *Jemeker, the wife of one of the biggest drug dealers in all of Los Angeles, had taken over the business all by herself and now she was single.* I was more than on the market; I was a walking target.

It's interesting to see how one man managed to get over the wall. I was at M & M restaurant when I saw a smooth, attractive dude pull up in a red Corvette. He had a shaved head and a diamond earring, he was clean, he was confident, and he had a look to him like he didn't play.

"Who's that?" I asked my cousin.

"Slick," she told me, staring at him as well.

I don't know if he had noticed me that day. The next time I saw him was at the car wash on Manchester and Van Ness. He was driving a truck just like Daff's and was dressed even finer than the first time I saw him. Everything about Slick said he had money.

As I was paying for my Platinum wash, which was a complete detail, he approached me and said, "Let me take care of that for you, Jemeker."

Not only does he notice me, he knows my name...

"You don't have to do that," I told him.

"I insist," he said.

"Do you know me?"

"I'd like to get to know you," he replied. "My name is Slick. Do you have any plans for this evening?" He continued, "I have two tickets to the Budweiser Superfest. I would love it if you would accompany me."

When he asked for my phone number, I told him I didn't give it out. "But you can give me yours," I said.

Like a whirlwind, Slick swept into my life and swept me off my feet. That evening, he took me to the

Budweiser Superfest at the Forum where the combination of the hot R&B and Slick's seductive charm had me feeling him.

Next thing I knew, he had me on a plane to Maui.

I had never been anywhere but L.A., Mississippi, and Las Vegas. Maui was paradise. Slick was a smooth operator; he arranged everything. He got the finest room at the finest hotel. Our bedroom opened on to the sand and the sea. At dinner, women in grass skirts danced in the ocean breezes as the sun went down behind the waves. When we hit the sheets, it was all about his lips. His techniques were like nothing I had ever experienced.

By the time we went home, I was hooked on Slick.

After Maui, the luxuries slowed down. It quickly became clear that Slick didn't have the money he pretended to have. But I did. I bought the man a mink coat, a diamond pinkie ring, and a Rolls-Royce. I was going to make him who I wanted him to be.

I also fronted him some work to get started. He had a friend in Oxnard who could move product. It didn't take long for business to pick up. Turned out the area was filled with college kids who loved our product.

In less than a month, we eloped to Las Vegas and married in the wedding chapel inside Circus Circus. Ironically, I married Slick in a chapel right across the street from where I had married Daff. I didn't go around broadcasting the fact that I'd married this man, but Slick bragged to everybody. When my friends and business partners found out, they didn't hold back their opinion of who this guy really was.

"He's deceitful and abusive to women!"

They didn't know what they were talking about; he was good to me and I couldn't get enough of him.

He told me, "You're all the woman I need!"

But my girl friend Sumer told me different.

"He's got women all over town!"

"My husband?" I asked, not believing her.

"I could name at least three other women, Jemeker. I'm telling you: Slick's no good!"

A couple other girl friends confirmed what Sumer had told me and even added to the list. The more my girls started telling me he was running around behind my back, the more I started turning him away in bed.

When I turned him away, Slick would get angry and tell me it was my duty to sleep with him. It was bad enough he was cheating, but now he thought he owned me.

Nobody owned me.

One day I got home and saw his feet on *my* couch, drinking juice *I'd* bought for Anthony out of one of *my* crystal glasses. I realized it was time to check him.

"Excuse me," I said. "Why are you drinking Anthony's juice? And get your feet off my couch with your shoes on!"

"I will put my feet wherever I want in this house and I'll drink Anthony's juice if I want to."

"Who do you think you're talking to?"

"I'm talking to you!" he shouted. "My wife! We're married! All this is mine!" Just to make his point, he threw the glass against the wall, shattering it. Then he stormed out.

Six months after we were together, my relationship with Slick was in trouble. We still had good business in Oxnard, but I was ready to walk away if things between us didn't improve.

Instead of improving, they only got worse.

One day while I was handling my affairs in L.A., I got into a car accident. I paged Slick to come pick me up but he didn't answer. I paged him again. Still nothing. Eventually I called a business associate, T, who picked me up and drove me back to Encino.

Slick pulled up as T was leaving.

"Who is that?" Slick yelled, and pulled his gun.

"Calm down!" I said. "I do business with him!"

When I looked in his eyes, I could see something wasn't right with him. I had my own gun nearby and, for a second, considered protecting myself. But then my common sense kicked in: this man was out of his mind with rage. A physical confrontation didn't make sense. I needed an escape route. I needed a way to calm him down. After he was calm, I could figure out a way to get him out of my life forever.

"Baby," I said softly, "I love you. I would never cheat on you. I know things have been a little rough, but I want to make it all better. No one can make love to me like you. You got the magic touch."

With that, I started kissing on Slick and leading him to the bedroom. My strategy was to play him with sex the way that he'd played me. If he had made a fool out of me, I'd make a bigger fool out of him.

The next morning, I called Johnny and told him to come over. When he arrived, I told him all about the drama I was having with Slick.

Johnny asked for his phone number and said he would take care of it. I don't know what Johnny said to him and I didn't care. I immediately filed for an annulment.

I moved out of the Encino house for good. Slick had played me and everyone knew it. I felt like a fool, I didn't want to see anybody and I didn't want anybody to see me. I didn't even want to be in the same town with Slick. I needed a change of scenery, a change of company, and a change of heart.

So I jumped on a plane and flew to Detroit.

Detroit wasn't just a city. Detroit was a man. Back around the time things were getting bad with Slick, I had gone to Las Vegas for a big championship boxing match. While there, I met a tall, handsome, and muscular fight promoter. I called him Detroit. By the way he carried himself in his elegant pin-striped business suit, I knew he had Game.

Detroit saw the same thing in me. He got me front-row seats to the bout and said, "Any time you want to come to the Motor City and get to know me better, let me know."

As soon as I got there, Detroit put Anthony and me up in a magnificent suite on the top floor of the brand-new Omni Hotel. As I settled in and looked across the river, I took a deep breath. The drama of the Slick situation was behind me. I was ready to get to know this new man.

Detroit proved himself to be every bit the gentleman. He treated both my son and me with the utmost respect. He took Anthony to Toys "R" Us and practically bought out the store. He sent flowers every day. At night, he took us to the finest restaurants.

For a month, Detroit never made any moves on me. I felt that we had a romantic connection, but he was interested in more than sex. Furthermore, he wasn't possessive and he wasn't trying to play me.

If anything, Detroit was just as controlled, smooth, and disciplined as I was. He kept his business life separate from his time with me. I knew he was a hustler and I knew he had connections, but he kept that on the down-low. The only people he introduced to me were his uncle and his best friend, both of whom had their game just as tight as his.

It also became clear that Detroit wasn't anyone to mess with. One time his uncle let it slip that Detroit had thrown his own cousin out of a second-story window after he didn't pay one of his debts. *His own cousin!* All of it made me wonder what kind of business tactics this man was using.

It wasn't long before I got my answer.

"So what do you do?" he asked me one night when the two of us were dining alone.

"I used to be married to a big drug dealer," I said, and left it at that.

"Do you know anybody in California who has product?"

I said yes, but I didn't tell him it was me. Just like he didn't tell me his business, I wasn't about to tell him mine.

Then I added, "When are you interested?"

"Right away," he said.

That night, I was on a plane to Los Angeles. And the next morning, I was back with fifty keys.

When I returned to the Omni, I rented two adjoining rooms. I put my workers who'd brought the dope in one room and met Detroit in the other. When he gave me the money, I went through the connecting door to the other room, got the dope, made the swap.

For the next two months, I made the most serious money of my life. I started flying back and forth almost every week for new shipments. Detroit moved whatever I gave him. And thanks to the price I was getting per key in Michigan compared to what I could get in California, I had forgotten about my problems in L.A.

Now I was with a man who treated me right, had his own money, and was helping me get even richer. My days of messing with the Slicks of the world were over. But even after two months, Detroit and I still hadn't slept together.

Was it me? Was it him?

I was putting out all the signs that I wanted Detroit, but he kept his guard up. And when I asked him to come back to L.A. with me for good, he said no.

"I got a woman here I don't want to disrespect, but I still want you to be my other woman," he said. "Don't worry, though. I'll take care of you."

To prove it, Detroit gave me money for a down payment on a house. But when he came out to L.A. two months later for some boxing business, he got his own room and wouldn't even come see the place I bought—a beautiful new three-bedroom house in Carlton Square, a gated community near the Forum.

I got the idea he didn't want to come into my world. "If you want to see somebody in L.A., I understand," he told me, "but just not when I'm here." Even then, though, he still kept things between us platonic, and the more he did, the more I wanted him. Several months later, he flew out to L.A. again, this time with his uncle.

One afternoon I was alone with his uncle, eating lunch in the hotel restaurant, while Detroit was taking a shower.

"How come Detroit never tries to get intimate with me?" I asked.

"Don't worry," he said. "That's your man."

But it had been almost a year and we still hadn't slept together.

I went to J.W. Robinson's in Beverly Hills and bought the sexiest lingerie ensemble I could find. The next time I saw Detroit, I was going to seduce him if it was the last thing I did.

That very night Detroit took me to a cozy restaurant—quiet table in the corner by a roaring fireplace, chateaubriand for two. Back at the suite, while Detroit relaxed in the living room, I excused myself for a few minutes. When I returned, I was wearing the seductive ensemble. It was made of pure silk; I felt irresistible! Detroit couldn't say no. Detroit didn't say no. He followed me to the bedroom, where, finally, we slept together. Unfortunately, my fantasy didn't quite come true. The lovemaking was not spectacular. I'd even have to call it ordinary. My woman's intuition told me that Detroit had made love not so much out of passion, but out of plain business sense.

In bed that night, I began to see the reality of our relationship. Detroit had no romantic interest in me. When he saw I had interest in him, he didn't want to push me away. He couldn't afford to push me away. So he went through the motions.

It was nothing but business.

But, hey, I was down with business. After all, I still hadn't revealed to Detroit that I was more than just a good connection. If he had kept his cool, to a large degree I had kept mine as well. I wasn't about to trip over a romance that would never happen.

The man made me *A LOT* of money. Having his business was good enough for me.

THE GAME IS CHANGING

I was in a downtown Atlanta club called Atlanta Nights. The DJ was bumping the sounds of the New Jack Swing and a thousand people were dancing on the floor. I was holding court in the VIP section, surrounded by ten of my best workers.

They weren't my workers in the drug game, though. These were ten fine-looking, young black women. And if you didn't notice their shiny, silky, full hair, they weren't doing their jobs right.

I wasn't in Atlanta on drug business. I was there for the Bronner Bros. International Hair Show, the biggest hair weave, product, and style convention in the world. My new business was in strong demand, thanks to the beautiful Italian hair I had begun to import and sell. Just like the drugs, I had the finest product money could buy.

It was also my birthday weekend. I'd been partying every night and hustling every day, making new connections in a new business that had me rising to the top of a whole new game.

How did I get there?

Let me rewind the story.

There's just something about black women and hair. To a black woman, a hair fashion means class and individuality. When it comes to hair, we're artistic, creative, and not afraid to show some style.

Daff never wanted me to have weaves, tracks, or extensions. Anything that wasn't part of me, he just didn't like. When I once got my hair done and came home with one small track in my hair, he noticed it immediately and made me take it out. But after Daff passed, I no longer had any limitations on what I could do; I was going to style my hair however I wanted.

I still wasn't sure what I was going to do with all my money. Since I'd taken over our business, nearly everybody who knew me outside the drug world asked one question more than any other:

"What do you do for a living?"

I would tell them I was in the bail bond business, which was partly true; I had posted quite a few bonds. But the one thing I didn't have was a real business.

The drug game was changing and I knew it wouldn't

last forever. I took out a pen and a pad and started brainstorming ideas. It was time for a legitimate business, but what?

The next day while getting my hair done, I asked my stylist James, "What is a good business to start?"

"Girl, you need to be selling hair," he replied.

James Gibson was the most exclusive black hair stylist in all of Los Angeles. He wove hair so beautifully it was impossible to tell where God's handiwork ended and his began. His client book read like a who's who of black Hollywood: Cicely Tyson, Stephanie Mills, Cherelle, and Jody Watley, just to name a few. James was pure style and class. He was also an excellent businessman, so when he made the suggestion, I took notice.

I started thinking about hair and how I could organize my business. I already knew I wanted to go right to the source; I needed a direct plug to the best hair money could buy. I'd never dealt with middlemen before and I wasn't about to start now. But I needed a connection.

James had told me the best hair came from Italy, so I knew that was where I had to go. I knew where Italy was on a map, but me in a foreign country, trying to find hair for sale? This was going to require some help. So I called the Italian embassy, asked the right questions, and got a directory for import-export companies and hair wholesalers. Then I called my girl friend Donna, who was in business school.

"Don't worry about money," I told her. "You just have to help me get where I'm going."

Shortly after that, we were on a plane bound for Paris, then a connecting flight to Milan. Milan was a city fit for a queen. The beautiful gallerias, the stone monuments, and high-class boutiques had my head spinning. Italian men swarmed Donna and me like we were celebrities, taking pictures and inviting us out everywhere we went.

When we didn't find the connection I needed in Milan, we took a plane to Palermo and hit the jackpot: warehouses full of thick, full, raw hair . . . hair in containers and washbasins, pretty little Italian women drying hair and sorting it into boxes and bins. Once I'd found a company I could do business with, I negotiated prices, made shipping arrangements, and put all the necessary pieces in place to start my supply line flowing. Before we left Italy, we went straight to another source—Gucci and Fendi—and shopped till we dropped.

Back home, I set up a corporation, rented an office near Centinella and Sepulveda, and Hair Distributors Inc. was established. But that wasn't the end of my business plan. I took speech classes at the Reading Game to develop proper English skills. I hired a trainer and started working out to be in the best of shape. In a few short months, I had crafted an entirely new image.

All my hard work paid off. James Gibson took me by the hand, said he'd be proud to be my escort, and began taking me around to all the most exclusive parties in L.A., introducing me as the woman with the best hair in town.

"Believe me," he'd tell everyone he knew, "this woman has the hair that glows and the hair that flows."

He wasn't exaggerating. No one could compete with my quality: not His and Her Hair Goods on Wilshire, not the Asian importers, *no one*. If you wanted the best hair money could buy, if you wanted natural hair that looked like your own, you came to Jemeker.

With my star on the rise and my reputation preceding me, my client book became just as prestigious as James's. One day, I would be at Cherelle's home. The next, I'd be going up the long, winding driveway to Berry Gordy's mansion in Bel Air to see his daughter-in-law.

"My name's Jemeker Mosley," I told the guard at the gate. "I'm here to see Karen Gordy."

It felt good to give the guard—an off-duty police officer—my driver's license. There I was, doing legitimate business at Berry Gordy's mansion. Mr. Gordy himself came in to check out the quality of my product and was impressed.

"I heard about you," he said. "Karen said you carry the best hair in town."

Berry Gordy knew who I was?

Right then, I realized I could be a star in any game I played.

My status didn't stop there, either. While I was building my reputation in the hair business, I became close friends with the late, great comedian Robin Harris. Robin was fascinated by me—even to the point that I became part of his stand-up routine.

"You watch," he told me, "I'm gonna make you a household name."

Robin created "Jamika" as a character in his routine called "Bébé's Kids." Jamika was the cool, beautiful woman who manipulated men into doing anything she wanted. "Bébé's Kids" became so popular, I became part of Robin's stage show.

"You don't believe that there really *is* a Jamika?" Robin would introduce me and I'd come onstage to bring him a glass of water. "Well here she is. Jamika!!"

The audience would applaud.

And I loved it.

Now I wasn't just a celebrity in the drug game and the hair business, I was a star in the public eye. And I flaunted it.

When I was partying in Atlanta, I'd have one of my girls walk up to the bouncer outside the club and tell him:

"This is Jamika from 'Bébé's Kids'!"

They'd open the velvet rope and let my whole entourage through. I'd walk straight in and go to the VIP section with my nose in the air like I owned the place.

It was during that same birthday weekend on that

same night that I caught the eye of another player in the Game—call him Atlanta.

Atlanta was a muscular, dark-skinned jewelry dealer that dressed well and had a nice smile. Atlanta pursued me romantically. He brought me to his jazz club, treated me and all my girl friends to dinner, and took me shopping. We became lovers.

After I flew back to L.A., he talked to me for hours on the phone and sent beautiful fresh flowers. Atlanta was also a true player. When we went into business, he proved he had the connections to move large quantities of product, handle his business professionally, and play the Game as well as Detroit.

Atlanta was cool.

Atlanta wasn't the only guy to whom I sold drugs in Atlanta. I had also met another man that weekend of the hair show—Basketball. I call him that because he was a star player abroad, but made his real money dealing drugs in the United States. With Basketball, I didn't need to use sex to keep him happy. He needed my drugs and enjoyed my company.

I was careful to keep Atlanta and Basketball from knowing that I was involved with both of them. I was finally getting good at keeping things straight. I had one man in Detroit selling my drugs and two other men in Atlanta doing the same. I still had money coming in all over L.A. My hair business was bigger than ever.

While I was jet-setting all over the country, partying

with Atlanta, Basketball, and Detroit, Anthony was at home, being raised by my mom. I would give him all the material things a little boy could ask for. But the truth was that I needed to be more of a presence in my son's life. Thanks to my success as a businesswoman, I was able to do so. We started doing everything together, from lavish birthday parties to skating every weekend to taking long, wonderful vacations.

On one occasion, we visited his father's grave.

Anthony asked, "Who killed my father?"

I had no answer.

"Why do you want to know, baby?" I asked.

"Because someday, I wanna get him."

"Don't worry. God'll take care of that," I said, and hugged and kissed my son.

Then my car phone rang. It was one of my workers. He called to tell me some friends of ours had been robbed and the entire family was murdered. The only one they found alive was their eight-month-old baby crawling around their twisted, lifeless bodies.

The drug game was changing fast. At one time, all the people that were robbing, stealing, and killing started selling drugs because the money was better. But whenever there was a dry spell and there were no drugs, they resorted back to what they used to do. And with the new laws, you got less time for robbing, stealing, and killing than you did for selling drugs.

It was open season on any drug dealers that were

doing well. And not just the dealers, their families too—women and children included. People were carjacked in broad daylight on main streets or kidnapped, tortured, and held for ransom. Some were released, some were murdered, whether the ransom was paid or not.

Jacking had become as popular as Vegas. If you hit the right drug dealer, you got the jackpot. Drug dealing had turned into something else. And I no longer wanted to be associated with it.

NO MISTAKES ALLOWED

Time was running out. But the Game kept pulling me in. The more I played, the more I made. The more money there was, the harder it was to get out.

One day I was downtown shopping at my favorite jewelry store when a sleek black limousine pulled up. A man in a red sweat suit climbed out and walked toward the store. As he reached for the door, they buzzed him in.

"I'm back, baby!" he shouted. "I need my stuff!"

Then he tapped me on the shoulder and asked, "Did you miss me?!"

"Excuse me?" I said, not recognizing him.

"It's Raphael!" he exclaimed.

I couldn't believe it. Back in the day, Raphael had been a major player. He was a good friend and associate of Daff's, who'd gone to jail right before Daff died. But that was five years ago. Since then, he'd lost two hundred pounds. Now, Raphael was all muscle.

As the salesperson came back with his jewelry, Raphael said, "Let's you and me talk, Jemeker. I heard some things that went down while I was in jail and I wanna straighten 'em out for you."

The next night, we had dinner at The Palm on Santa Monica, a high-priced hangout for show business stars and movie moguls.

"I was sorry to hear about Daff," he said as we ate lobster. "He was a good dude. Everybody loved him."

"I miss him every day," I said as we toasted his memory.

"But I couldn't understand how you'd ever go with a buster like Slick," Raphael continued. "Dude isn't right. Just give me the word and I'll handle it."

"Before we parted, I left a couple keys in Oxnard that I never got paid for. I don't want any blood on my hands, but I do want my money," I told Raphael.

"Gimme his number," Raphael said with a smile.

Not long after that, Slick called me.

"Why'd you give Raphael my number?" he said. "I thought me and you were straight."

"I don't know how you thought that," I said, and hung up the phone.

Slick called me right back. "Just tell me what I owe you—"

"Deal with Raphael," I told him, and hung up again.

That weekend, Raphael took me to a club on Crenshaw and Imperial where Slick was known to hang out.

Raphael and I hit the dance floor and started having a good time. Later, I saw Slick come in, then watched as Raphael's boys surrounded him. I don't know what they said, but Slick turned around and left immediately. And the next day, Raphael was back at my house with my money.

Raphael made it clear that he saw me as more than a friend. He kept on asking me out. Then came the day when he was at my house.

"You know, Jemeker," he said, "Daff always bragged on you. I never made a move on you, out of respect, but don't think I didn't want to."

"C'mon, Raphael," I said, "stop playing. We're like family."

"Well, I'm not playing. And I got ten thousand dollars behind how I feel. I want you."

I never really looked at him that way, but if he was willing to give me ten thousand dollars, I was willing to take it.

From there, Raphael became a business associate and a lover on the down-low. I had other men and he had other women, but they weren't problems. Just like with

Detroit, Atlanta, and Basketball, Raphael knew it was always money first.

Raphael's territory was Oakland, which added richly to my out-of-town business. For a while, we did steady runs with Raphael taking the product up the coast and returning with the cash.

One day, looking at the news, I couldn't believe what I saw: there was Raphael on the side of the highway in handcuffs. I even got up close to the screen to make sure. It was him all right.

My heart started racing.

A little while later, Raphael called. He gave me the name he was arrested under and where he was being held so I could post his bail. But before I could bail him out, his fingerprints gave away his true identity and the fact that he was on parole sent him back to prison.

A few weeks later, James Gibson called. He was at a recording studio in Hollywood with one of his celebrity friends and invited me over.

When I walked in, I couldn't help but notice the soothing voice of the R&B singer.

"Who is that?" I asked. "He sounds good."

James's friend asked, "Do you want to meet him?"

"Yes," I replied.

When we went into the control room, I saw a tall, light-skinned brother with boyish good looks.

James's friend made the introduction: "Jemeker, meet the next Marvin Gaye."

"Just call me Cheez," said the singer.

I sat there for the rest of the evening, listening to this man put his romantic heart into every note.

Later that night, we were getting to know each other over chicken and waffles at Roscoe's on Sunset and Gower. Cheez was from St. Louis and commuted back and forth while he worked on his music career. He was also a drug dealer.

There was something about his sweet, lighthearted charm and joking good humor that put me at ease. Cheez wasn't like other drug dealers I knew: he wasn't hard like Raphael, cold like Slick, or distant like Detroit. He was funny and he adored me.

Cheez showered me with attention. He'd pick me up in his Corvette, put down the top, and cruise on up the coast. He'd sing Johnny Gill and Luther Vandross love songs all the way to Malibu, inserting my name whenever he could. We'd eat crab and lobster at Gladstone's. Other times, we'd drive all the way to Santa Barbara to stay at the Miramar. We'd rent mopeds and jog the beach. When it came to lovemaking, Cheez was fantastic. He had Slick's technique—and then some.

Cheez became part of my professional and business life. He took product to sell in St. Louis, opening still another market for me. And he also managed to get me to do something I swore I'd never do again: fall in love.

But this time, it was different. I had Detroit, Atlanta, and Basketball. They were like drawers in a desk—I could open and close them whenever I wanted to. I was in control. But I also realized I needed to leave the Game; I needed to concentrate solely on hair.

As you can imagine, though, hair was one hundredth as profitable as drugs. So I kept delaying a precise exit strategy. I couldn't see myself walking away from all that money. That was one drawer I was still unable to close.

When it came to Cheez, I thought he was strong both in business and music. I thought he had it all together. But, like they say, love is blind. I realized that when one day Cheez and I took a group of our friends to Magic Mountain. It was a beautiful spring afternoon. It was all about having fun on the rides. Cheez was the best possible companion at an amusement park because he turned into a ten-year-old child. I loved that about him.

But on this day he seemed too silly, too wired. His energy wasn't right. He was talking nonstop and acting goofy. When we stopped at a concession stand to eat, he reached in his pocket, pulled out some money, and a small plastic bag fell out. As I picked it up I saw it was cocaine.

"What are you doing with this?" I asked him.

"It's not mine," he said.

"It's in your pocket."

"I'm just holding it for someone else," he replied.

"Yeah, right!"

His lying to me was one thing; I could handle that. Men had lied to me before; that's what men did. But using—getting high on your own supply—that was something else.

That was a sign of weakness. And one thing you learn in the Game is that one weak link can destroy an entire chain. I could never afford to be weak in any area. The relationship was over.

ON THE RUN

I'd already been transitioning out of the drug business, but discovering Cheez's habit was a wake-up call.

So much for a precise exit strategy; it was time to pull the plug.

Time to get out of the drug game for good.

Though I remained on good terms with everyone I did business with, I pulled away from my sources and stopped selling to my customers. I had to make Hair Distributors Inc. my number one priority.

Each year I'd been in the hair business, I threw a lavish fashion show. Hundreds of people attended, from the best and the brightest hair stylists in Los Angeles to the many celebrities I knew. The gala affair was the perfect venue to highlight the different styles of hair I sold, as well as the different ways the hair could be used. Most of all, it was a very good way to promote my business.

June 23, 1991, I filled the Los Angeles Hilton's biggest ballroom. My last hair show the hilariously talented comedian Martin Lawrence had the audience in stitches, but this year Simply Marvelous had us on the floor and I laughed so hard I was in tears, and the beautiful R&B singer Miki Howard serenaded the crowd. Even though Cheez and I were no longer together professionally or romantically, he sang a beautiful ballad. There were no hard feelings between us.

The main event was an elaborate production to rival any runway fashion show I had ever seen. I used all the same models I brought to Atlanta and then some. I had a whole team of professionals to handle wardrobe, makeup, and hair. I developed a theme for the presentation—luxury and elegance.

At the end of the evening, Anthony came out in a little tuxedo, introduced me, and read a speech thanking everyone for coming. I made my entrance wearing a diamond tiara and a dress made entirely of shiny, black hair. The crowd gave me a standing ovation.

The show built up my business and pumped up my ego. It also helped me forget I was ever in the drug game.

I could and would be the queen of anything I set my mind to.

One day, Cheez's sister called from Alton, Illinois. She mentioned that one of her daughters had been arrested at the train station. She'd probably been picking up a delivery, but I didn't think anything of it. Cheez didn't buy his drugs from me anymore. Instead, he did his business with a Dominican connection. The drugs involved in the bust couldn't be traced back to me.

Then I heard Cheez got arrested. I still wasn't concerned, though. I'd been out of the Game for so long, I thought I was safe.

But was I?

I was getting ready to go to the office one morning when Linda, my assistant, called.

"The FBI was just here."

"What did they say?"

"They were looking for you."

I hung up the phone. I didn't know what they were there for, but I did know they were looking for me. And I wasn't going to speak to them until I had more information.

I started thinking, *Cheez had just gotten arrested, was he snitching?*

I knew he was the weak link! Right then and there, I started packing my things. Not just my things, but Anthony's things and Clifton's things as well. When I was finished, I stuffed as much as I could fit into my Maxima and drove straight to my mother's house.

Anthony and Clifton had rooms set up at my mother's house, same as they had at mine. To them, going back and forth was nothing out of the ordinary.

I kissed my son good-bye and told him I'd be back soon.

But I told my mother, "I've got to go away for a while."

She didn't ask questions.

And I didn't give details.

I told my secretary the same thing that I told my mother. I also instructed my secretary to run the business in my absence. After putting my affairs in order, I went to a friend's house. I needed a few days to get my thoughts together and figure out my next move.

A few days turned into a few months. I stayed inside during daylight hours. Since my friend wouldn't take my money, I scrubbed her floors, washed her windows, vacuumed, dusted, cooked meals...anything to occupy my time.

At night, I'd slip out to pick up the money from the hair business. I ran errands. And when my chores were done, I'd sneak into my mom's house and crawl into bed with my son. If he woke, I hugged him and kissed him, told him I loved him, and rocked him back to sleep.

When I'd call my mom from a pay phone, she'd tell me when the Feds had come around. I knew she was safe because she wasn't lying when she said she didn't know where I was or what I was doing.

I also changed my identity with a new driver's license and social security card. I purchased two cell phones and used them only for outgoing calls. And I never called anyone I thought the Feds might be watching.

I made certain no one could find me.

The only other person who knew my whereabouts was my brother Johnny. Whenever I'd talk to him, he'd tell me everything was going to be okay.

"Keep running," he said, "and you'll be fine."

After six months, the Feds stopped coming by Mom's house. Up to then, I knew to lay low and keep in hibernation, but now the heat was off.

Time to escape Los Angeles.

I took a cab to the airport one night, paid cash for a one-way red-eye ticket to Alabama, and, just like that, I was gone.

On the other end, I had someone waiting for me at the airport, a man I'll call Birmingham. He was a recruiter for Alabama State University, whom I'd met at a Bronner Bros. hair show. Though we hadn't ever dated, we'd developed a friendship and had kept in touch. He had no idea I was on the run.

Birmingham was a wonderful guy who lived a square life. We became lovers as well as friends. I moved into his comfortable little house near the university, where I cooked our meals and kept our life orderly. If there were college games at night or on the weekends, we went. I slept easy knowing I didn't need to look over my shoulder every five minutes. Alabama was a safe hiding place.

I knew, though, that I couldn't stay forever. I missed Anthony and I couldn't bear the pain of being separated from him. I kept my feelings locked up inside, but when I was alone I'd break down and cry like a baby.

One evening, Birmingham and I went to a lovely dinner. The food, the warm autumn evening air—everything was right. But everything was also wrong because I was so far away from my son.

I needed someone to talk to, so I picked up the phone and called my best friend, Tynia, who had by then become a minister. I cried my heart out to her.

"Jemeker," she said, "you need to turn yourself in."

I wasn't in any mood to hear what she had to say. I was angry at God and the whole world for keeping me from my son and I wasn't about to consider surrendering as an option.

No matter what, I was still in control.

As summer came around, I couldn't stand it any longer. I couldn't stand being away from my son. I had to go back to L.A. I flew home and went straight to my friend's house. I told my mom I was back, and went to pick up Anthony one day after day camp.

"Baby," I said as I grabbed him in my arms, "you're coming home with me."

I took out a line of credit on my new identity and bought a town house in Westchester, near the airport. I took Anthony to the YMCA day camp every morning and picked him up every afternoon. We did everything together: waterslides, mini golf, Malibu Grand Prix, parks, and picnics—anything he wanted. With my son back in my life, it was a lovely summer.

"It's you and me against the world," I told him. "Ride or die."

That summer, there was another man. I'll call him Westchester. He was a real estate broker I met at the gym. I never told Westchester who I really was; I never let him get close. Though we enjoyed our time together, he became another drawer I could open and close whenever necessary.

When Anthony's school year began, I left him with Mom again, closed the drawer on Westchester, and reopened Birmingham. It was time to take a vacation to Alabama. Birmingham was happy to see me. Life on the run was beginning to feel normal.

But was I happy?

In my mind, I was convinced I was enjoying life. But deep down, the chaos and the drama were getting to me. Whenever I returned to L.A., I couldn't lead a normal life because of the Feds. When I was out of town, I could live the way I wanted, but was away from Anthony.

I kept running.

Back to Michigan to see Detroit, who was no longer my business partner or lover, but just a friend.

Then back to Atlanta, where I had my choice of several men.

Then over to Miami, where still another man, with whom I'd done drug business, was happy to see me.

Back and forth, running, running, running.

The men paid my bills and helped me keep up my lifestyle. But my lifestyle couldn't support my spirit. My spirit was declining. Inside, I felt myself falling apart.

The only person I could truly talk to was Tynia. I continued to call her and she continued to tell me about God.

"He's trying to tell you something, Jemeker."

"I don't want to hear about God!" I'd tell her over and over again. "If God is really God, why is he trying to take me from my son?!"

Tynia never pointed out how my own mistakes had gotten me where I was. She never preached. No matter how many times I went off on her, she was gentle and kind. And when I was through crying into the phone, Tynia would still be there, calmly praying for me.

I wasn't ready to believe that God could tell me anything. But I knew something had to give.

TALKING FOR FREE

It was my decision to go to Anthony's graduation. Now I was handcuffed in the back of an unmarked car, riding with two FBI agents. I slid down the seat; I didn't want to be seen. But as I glanced out the window over the city that I loved, it looked very different to me. It was as though I was seeing it for the first time. My mind began to ask questions:

What had I done to myself?

Where were they taking me?

What did they really know?

What evidence did they have?

I knew I'd never been caught with any drugs!!

Whatever they had, I wasn't worried. I had money to hire the best attorneys to beat my case.

I was taken to a building downtown and driven underground. I couldn't help but notice the fully armed police looking like a SWAT team.

All this for me?

Who did they think I was? Al Capone?

I was escorted inside, uncuffed, and put into a holding cell.

The guard said, "Welcome to Metropolitan Detention Center."

Many hours later, I was taken to another floor, fingerprinted, photographed, and processed. Then I was moved to an adjacent room where I was stripped of my designer clothes, then searched. It was one of the most degrading and humiliating things I had ever experienced. I was given some khakis and some dingy underwear that looked like it should have been thrown away twenty years ago. I put on the khakis but there was no way on God's green earth that I was going to put on somebody else's underwear.

By 2:00 a.m. I was alone in a tiny cell with two bunk beds. I hadn't eaten anything since yesterday morning. I had no blanket and no pillow and it was freezing. I tried to sleep on my hands to keep warm but there was no escaping the cold.

At 5:00 a.m. the lights came on and my cell door opened with a *CLANK* that startled me.

A guard told me, "It's chow time!"

I was hungry, but I was more interested in calling Mom.

When my mother asked if I was okay, I told her, "I'm hungry and it's freezing in here!"

"They're not feeding you?" she asked.

"Yeah, they're serving breakfast right now."

"Well, you need to eat," my mother said. "Bless your food, call me back when you finish, and pray for God to keep you warm."

Instead, I prayed, *God, get me out of this mess.*

When I prayed, I felt God's presence. I had always felt God's presence over me, even when I was delivering drugs. Now that I was in jail, I couldn't understand why he'd allowed me to be captured in the first place. Looking back, I had a limited understanding of who God truly was, but I was sure he would get me out.

After I prayed, I called one of the city's top defense attorneys I'd retained in case I ever got caught.

When we were face-to-face, the lawyer told me, "You're being charged with conspiracy to distribute cocaine and money laundering."

"Just post my bail as soon as possible," I told him. "I don't want to spend another night in this place."

But I ended up spending another night at MDC and then another one until a week had passed.

A week of not knowing what was going to happen to me.

A week of hell.

Every night, I had the same horrible nightmare: I saw Anthony crying in front of his school as the Feds took me away. Each time, there was nothing I could do about it.

As bad as the week was, I remained confident. If I

hadn't been arraigned yet, it was because they couldn't build a case against me. Ever since I'd started selling weed on Twelfth Avenue, I'd been the most careful person I knew. I had the best lawyer in town and my mother was ready to post bail as soon as they gave me one. Whatever the amount, I wanted out of there.

Those were my thoughts when I went before a Los Angeles federal judge for a preliminary hearing. In the courtroom, I made eye contact with my mother and family and gave them a determined look that said I was in control of the situation—*don't worry.* Right up to the moment my attorney requested bail, I was certain I'd be a free woman by the end of the day.

But my bail was denied. I was being extradited to St. Louis.

Cheez!

After a month at MDC, I was taken to a military airfield and put on a prisoner transport plane. This was the furthest thing from the private charters and first-class experiences I was used to. Instead of a sleeper seat, I was shackled and chained. Instead of lobster and champagne, I was given a sack lunch. Instead of my friends and family, I was surrounded by hundreds of federal prisoners and criminals.

During the long flight, some said hi and tried to make small conversation, but I had nothing to say. I didn't know these people, and, as far as I was concerned, we had nothing in common.

When we finally landed in St. Louis, I was transported to a small county jail outside of town. If L.A.'s MDC was bad, this place was ten times worse. Imagine *Mayberry R.F.D.* with no Aunt Bee and you'll have the Greenville, Illinois, county jail. It was drafty and had the stench of urine and waste.

My meals consisted of the same thing every day: a bowl of Froot Loops for breakfast, a bologna sandwich for lunch, and a TV dinner at night. The only thing to supplement my diet were Snickers and potato chips from the vending machine. Worst of all, the faucets and pipes were so rusty the water came out brown. For the whole time I was there, all I had to drink was the little plastic bottles of fake Kool-Aid I was given with the peel-off foil top.

A month passed. My relatives in Missouri would come to visit on weekends, but I still had no idea what was going on or when I would have my freedom back.

One day, a guard told me I had a visitor. Expecting my family, I thought I'd be going to the visitation room, but instead I was escorted into a small, windowless cell. A strange man came in and started asking questions about who I knew and who I'd done business with. At first he pretended to be friendly, but then his mood changed. He said if I didn't answer his questions I'd be looking at twenty-five to life and I'd never see my son again.

I told him, "I'm not answering any of your questions

and I will see my son! But I don't ever want to see you again! This visit is over!"

After that, I refused any visit that wasn't my lawyer or family.

When I called my lawyer in Los Angeles, I asked what could be done about a new bail hearing. He told me he was going to start calling law firms in St. Louis.

"You need an attorney who's licensed to practice in Missouri."

I ended up with an attorney named Scott, a novice lawyer fresh out of law school. I was his first federal case, but friends, associates, and the L.A. lawyer reassured me that a young lawyer would work hard and have more time for me. So I hired Scott as my lawyer and started to build my defense.

In the discovery process, I learned that Cheez's and his family's testimony was all the government had to go on. This increased my optimism; between Cheez's drug addiction and the simple fact that he and his co-informants were related, I knew we could discredit them. The D.A.'s office was trying to get more people to testify but I couldn't imagine anyone else coming forward. I had always been extremely careful of the company I'd kept and had always taken care of my people. I knew there were new conspiracy laws, but I didn't think they applied to me.

I was more confident than ever.

My lawyer wasn't so sure.

"Jemeker," he said one day, "I'm going to be honest with you. Based on the new law, the government has a case. You *ARE* going to get some time no matter what."

Even after he showed me the law on paper and tried to explain it as best he could, I refused to believe him.

"They're offering you a deal," he continued. "They'll give you the lowest end of an eight-year sentence, but you've got to cooperate. Do you know anything?"

I knew what he was really asking me:

Did I know other people I could turn on?

Would I tell on my friends and business associates?

I wasn't about to break the rules of the Game, not then or ever. So I looked Scott in the eye and told him, "I don't know anything."

"Then the only other choice is to go to trial," he said.

After six months, my case finally went to trial. My family was there to support me. I wore nice suits to court. I held my head high.

Finally, I'm going to get out of here.

I had read everything in discovery and thought I knew the ins and outs of the prosecution's case. I knew where Cheez had told half-truths and entire lies. I was ready to defend myself and rebut anything he said.

On the first day of court, I was in a downtown

St. Louis holding cell, waiting for the proceedings to begin, when a guy in an adjacent cell said, "You're Jemeker, right?"

I said I was.

He explained that Cheez and he were codefendants in another case. "I've never met you but I know who you are. And I want you to know something: Cheez told on me too! They wanted me to testify against you but I'm not doin' it. I'm not goin' out like that."

There it was—the code of the street in full effect. God was looking out for me. I saw this man's words as another sign that I couldn't lose.

The first few days of the trial were filled with legal hearings, technical motions, and the jury selection process. It concerned me that there were no black people selected to hear my case, but I still felt I was going home. When Cheez took the stand, he avoided eye contact. But when they asked him to point me out in the courtroom, he didn't hesitate. When asked if I had personally sold him drugs, he said I had. He claimed I knew the Dominicans he did drug business with—that wasn't true. A lot of other things he said during his testimony were not true. I let Scott know all of this for cross-examination purposes.

With each new lie, I looked at Cheez and I thought: *How can you sit there—sworn to tell the truth—and disrespect me?*

I can't believe this dude!

Just because you got caught now you wanna tell on everybody you know—destroying their lives and their families—how could I have fallen for such a sucka?!

And for what—so you can save yourself?

This is YOUR case! Take it like a man!

I didn't just hate Cheez for what he was doing.

I wanted to kill him.

I couldn't wait for cross-examination!!

The rest of Cheez's family was just as pathetic. His brother, his two nieces, and every friend and relative that testified on his behalf said they saw me sell him drugs.

Then the bomb dropped: Cassandra walked into the courtroom. Cassandra had been my secretary at the hair business. I had no idea that she'd been called by the prosecution. When she got on the stand, she testified that I'd asked her to deliver drugs to Cheez.

My heart stopped.

How could she turn on me like this? After all I'd done for her! I'd given her a job, paid her under the table, and even given her a car to get to work! And this was the thanks I got? She didn't even have a case! She was talking for free! She went out backward for a bus ticket to Missouri!

But what she said was true.

I kept waiting for Scott to discredit everyone in his cross-examinations. I was waiting for him to point out all the inaccuracies I had spotted in their testimonies.

But he was outmaneuvered by an experienced D.A.

who was very comfortable in the courtroom. During the closing arguments, the D.A. made a forceful case. He made it plain that the new law said that I didn't have to be caught with drugs; it was enough to prove that I was involved in the drug trade. He linked me to a large criminal conspiracy to sell cocaine and launder money. He accused me of perjury. He said I destroyed lives and manipulated and conned people. He made me out to be a major player in the drug world.

He called me the "Queen Pin."

I didn't see myself that way at all.

In my mind, I was just a good businesswoman.

The jury was excused and I was sent back to a holding cell. As I waited for the verdict to come in, I still believed I would be found innocent. I was still convinced that the jury would set me free.

The prosecution's entire case was built on hearsay.

A few hours later, November 15, 1993, the verdict came in and trial was reconvened. As I was led into the courtroom, I made eye contact with Anthony and blew him kisses. I mouthed the words "I love you" and looked forward to holding him again.

Right up to the moment the verdict was read aloud, I fully expected I'd be with my son that afternoon.

"Guilty on all counts."

I was traumatized.

Anthony began to cry.

After my sentencing date was set for April 22, 1994,

the judge looked at my son, looked at me, and said to the bailiffs:

"Let them talk."

I held my baby as he cried. I told him how much I loved him. I told him to be strong.

Then they took me away.

SET FREE

On the ride back to what had been home for the last few months, I was *DISGUSTED.* Between that jury, which hadn't included *ANY* of my peers, and that dump truck of a lawyer, I didn't have a chance.

I still believed my verdict would be overturned. I would hire a new attorney, file an appeal, and have my case retried.

After the trial, Anthony and my mother came to visit me every day for a week. Though I was happy to be reunited with the two most important people in my life, it was bittersweet. It hurt my heart that my mother and son had to experience being locked in a prison cell to visit me. I often wanted to cry, but I didn't—I enjoyed our visits. We played checkers and cards and talked about everything but the trial.

Our time together was a bright light in a dark time of my life.

"Mom," I told her before she and Anthony left,

"some of what they said in court was true, but not all of it. I just want you to know that."

"I know," she said. "I'll talk to you later."

Knowing my mother believed in me made me feel better.

After they were gone, I read the letters my friends and family had written to the judge on my behalf. They went to great lengths to say how I was generous and kind. They described me as an upstanding member of my community.

On one hand, I was the person they said I was. But they didn't know the other life I lived. In my mind, I'd done a lot of wrong for the right reason. But, whatever the reason, wrong is wrong.

It was especially hard to read the letter my mother had written. In her letter, she mentioned:

"... Losing my daughter is like losing my right arm."

Reading that letter brought tears to my eyes. Not only had my bad decisions hurt myself, but, worst of all, they had hurt the ones I loved. From that day forward, I would be more responsible for making better decisions.

Right then, I needed to find a new lawyer.

When I contacted my L.A. lawyer, he told me I couldn't hire another attorney until after sentencing. He also added that I had been misrepresented and I should report Scott to the Missouri State Bar Association. I tried to get in touch with Scott, but when I called his office, they told me he was no longer with the firm.

No longer with the firm?!

Well, where is he?!

Who's going to prepare my case for sentencing?!

I can't hire another lawyer until after my sentencing!

Once again, I was on my own. As if I didn't have enough problems, the D.A.'s office was still harassing me, trying to get me to cooperate. They'd tell me they could reduce my sentence. They even offered me a deal, saying it would get me back home to my son. As much as I wanted to be with my son, telling was not an option.

Between the stress, diet, and unsuitable drinking water, I became ill. I lost a substantial amount of weight, my face broke out, and my body ached all over. The prison staff finally took me to receive medical attention. The doctor never touched me, he just looked at me and said I had a bladder infection, gave me some meds, and told me I needed to drink more water. When I got back to the jail, I spoke to the sheriff. I asked him if they could take money off my books to buy bottled water to drink and take my medication. He said yes.

Months later, Scott finally showed up. He wasn't alone. I immediately dug in on him: "Where have you been?!"

Instead of answering, he introduced the man he had brought. The guy was from presentencing and was there to interview me. The interview was extensive. After the man left, I started back in on Scott: "What happened at my trial?! Why didn't you do what the L.A. lawyer said?!"

"I was listening to the people at my firm," he replied. "I'm sorry—I'm really sorry."

Scott was younger than me, but looked a lot older. He looked bad. He looked like he'd had a nervous breakdown. He told me he had quit the firm right after my trial. It seemed that my case had destroyed his career. My anger turned to sympathy. I found myself thanking him for his honesty.

A half hour later, a guard escorted me to chapel. When I arrived, a white preacher in his early thirties was ministering to the room of inmates. There was something different about this man; I could feel the peace and sincerity in his voice.

When he said, "Is there anyone that wants to receive the Holy Spirit?" I wanted to receive whatever he had!

I raised my hand. The preacher approached and anointed my head with oil. As soon as he laid his hand on me, I began to speak, but not in a language I could understand. Words cannot describe the feelings of happiness, joy, and love. It was a wonderful encounter. As he laid his hands on others, they also received the Holy Spirit.

Then he walked over to a silver tub and said, "Whoever wants to be baptized, please come forward!"

I did. I needed to be cleansed. When I was lifted out of the water, my hands were in the position of prayer. I began to speak in my new language, but this time I knew exactly what I was saying.

FORGIVENESS

I went back to my cell, a baby in Christ, excited and full of joy and love from my encounter.

I got on my bunk, knelt on my knees, pulled the covers up over my head, and began to pray. My prayer was a searching and fearless confession of my sins. For each one, I asked God's forgiveness:

Forgive me for lying about being a drug dealer...

Forgive me for the lives I've destroyed...

Forgive me for putting my son's life in jeopardy...

Forgive me for the people I've hurt...

Forgive me for using the men I've been with...

Sins I had totally forgotten came back to me. Things I would never repeat to another human being I gave up to God for forgiveness.

I remained in confession through the night and into the next morning. God's presence was all around me. I wasn't tired or emotional; I was relaxed and at peace. I poured myself out to the Lord and when I was finished, I felt the unburdening of his forgiveness. As I let his love wash over me, I prayed that the people I'd hurt would forgive me too.

By 6:00 a.m. I was elated. I had such zeal for my new grace, I got on the phone and began to spread the good news:

My friend Sonya was absolutely thrilled.

"It's this language coming out of me," I told her. "I can't explain it but I love it!!"

Westchester, who had become a minister by then, was equally excited. But Tynia was most excited of all. Her prayer for my salvation had been answered.

Everyone I spoke with counseled me to read my Bible. I began immediately. Right from the beginning, verses jumped out, speaking straight to my life experience. Just by chance I turned to Jeremiah 31:34:

> *"I will forgive their iniquity, and I will remember their sin no more."*

Words I couldn't pronounce or understand made sense. With each new passage, scripture replenished my soul. It became food in my hunger for spiritual growth. I studied from the moment I woke until the lights went out. I read the Bible from Genesis to Revelation in three months.

Then I began to read it again. I rejoiced in God's

teachings. I started learning verses then stories. Though I found wisdom in every Bible story I read, there were four that touched my spirit with special meaning: Joseph, Jonah, Job, and Jesus's encounter with the woman at the well.

When Joseph's father showed him favor, his brothers turned against him and threw him in a well. Then he was sold into slavery among his enemies. Even though he was forced into isolation and taken from the people he loved, God took care of him and put him in the favor of his captors. When his wisdom and generosity earned him his freedom, Joseph returned to his family not only with forgiveness, but with salvation from famine.

Even though his brothers turned on him, as Cheez had turned on me, Joseph never showed anything but kindness. How could I remain angry with Cheez? If Joseph could forgive and if God had forgiven *me,* then I could and would forgive my own enemies. Furthermore, God showed me how I would someday be freed to return with new spiritual strength to help those in need.

As for Jonah, I learned that one day was like a thousand years and a thousand years was like one day in the eyes of God. When Jonah refused God's commandments and tried to flee his word, he was swallowed up by the whale. When he found prayer and submitted to God's will for him, he was spit out into the light of day, only to rise to far greater glory and carry God's message to the people of Nineveh.

Like Jonah in the belly of the whale, I realized that no matter how long I was locked in jail, it was like the blink of an eye compared to being locked in the bondage of self. Being blind to the light of God was far worse than any prison. I thought back to my former life and realized that I'd been in darkness. But having been spit out, I had surrendered to a new way of life. Though my time was dark in the earthly sense, I had faith that one day there would be light. And no matter what, I knew that God had a purpose for me.

A prosperous man, Job had his whole world taken from him as a test of his faith. Even after his children, his livelihood, and his health were gone, he never cursed God or blasphemed his name. Though I had been angry with God when I knew no better, I had never cursed him either. And with my new faith, I would not blaspheme his name now.

In my current situation, I took great comfort and found wisdom in Job's words to his wife:

"Shall we accept good from God, and not trouble?"

Like Joseph, Jonah, and Job, I saw the tremendous power of faith. Their stories related to being alone and isolated. I saw all three men jailed, yet I also saw how God had taken care of them in the midst of extraordinary circumstances. I started to see how their experiences with loneliness had reinforced their relationship with God.

By taking me out of the life I'd known, God was building me up in my faith. Only in loneliness could I learn to depend on something greater than myself. By breaking me down, God was saying:

"I love you, but you don't know everything."

"I love you, but you didn't create the universe."

"I love you, but you aren't in control."

"I love you, but everyone and everything else has failed you. Now what are you going to do?"

Reading those Bible stories, I could see God's presence in my own life. This was especially true with the fourth story: the woman at the well. Like her, I had been cast out for my sins. I had been with many men and lived by carnal pleasures. Like her, I had been shown by God the need to confess my sins before I could receive the life-giving waters of salvation and grace. And like her, I had met God face-to-face in my loneliness and felt his arms wrap around me.

With renewed spirit, the woman at the well went forth to lead many conversions in the name of God. Like her, I craved the opportunity to put my faith into works and actions, to be a different woman from the one who had been put in a cell.

I went to Bible study at Vandalia whenever I could. I went to church for spiritual fellowship with anyone and everyone. I comforted the occasional women who'd pass through, mostly girls with DUIs or shoplifting charges. They'd cry and I'd let them know that they were going to be all right, doing my best to give them some peace.

In my own studies, I continued to see my past for what it was. There was humility and patience that came from accounting for things that I never wanted to experience again. There was much pride, shame, and pain. But God broke it all down and replaced it with love, joy, and kindness.

In Greenville, I got close to one of the ladies who would come in from a local church and minister to me.

"You have a gift of compassion, Jemeker," she told me. "You should be witnessing to other inmates."

Since I was the only woman in Greenville, I began working with the guys. I also encountered an old white man named Lloyd, who was a part-time guard.

"What are you reading?" he asked one day when he came to deliver my breakfast.

"The Bible," I said.

"I don't believe in that stuff," he growled, and moved on.

The next time he saw me, he asked, "You still reading that Bible?"

I smiled and said, "I sure am."

A few weeks later, he asked, "How's your Bible today?"

Over the next few months, Lloyd softened up. He'd sneak me fresh apples and tell me about his farm. As we got to know each other, we became friends.

Then one day, he asked, "Will you read your Bible to me?"

I did so with great joy in my heart. Lloyd admitted that even though he'd been Christian, he'd never given himself to God. Before the day was over, I had led him through the Sinner's Prayer and back to a relationship with God.

It gave me great happiness to know that I helped lead Lloyd to the Lord. I saw how even I, a baby in Christ, could pour out his message to others. I was delighted that God had decided to use me.

My sentencing date finally arrived. It had been six months since I'd been convicted, but it felt like a lifetime.

In the days leading up to my hearing, I fasted, cleansing my body as I cleansed my soul. I was facing the possibility of twenty-five to life.

I prayed for a miracle.

I'll admit that a big part of me was still expecting God to save me from my mess.

The night before the hearing, I couldn't sleep. As I read the story of Jesus in the garden from the book of Matthew, I saw his own prayer to God in the face of his own trial:

> *"Oh my Father, if it be possible, let this cup pass from me: Nevertheless not as I will but as you will."*

I asked God: "If you can do a miracle to get me out of this mess, I'll serve you till the day I die." Looking back, I see how I was trying to cut a deal with God—*You give me this and I'll give you that.*

The morning of sentencing, I got in the van and rode downtown. When I got there, I waited in the holding cell, got dressed, and, when I was called, walked into the courtroom. My family from Missouri was there. So was Scott the lawyer.

When the D.A. spoke, his words were harsh and clear. He said I was a Queen Pin, a menace to society. He said I had ruined families and destroyed lives.

As he spoke, I listened to his words with a straight face and the startling knowledge that it was me he was talking about. The whole time he spoke, I silently prayed: *God, be with me in my hour of public shame.*

When judgment was passed, I received 180 months. It took me a while to add it up, but when I did, I realized that fifteen years was on the low end of the sentencing guidelines. Everyone in the federal system does 85 percent of his or her time, but that still meant thirteen years.

On the van ride back to jail, I was happy, but it was bittersweet. On one hand, I knew my time and it was one less thing to worry about. On the other hand, even though I'd received the low end of the guidelines, thirteen years was still thirteen years.

In my lack of perfect faith, I still hoped that God

would stop the van, remove my shackles and chains, and allow me to walk free.

But I knew it didn't work that way.

So instead, I prayed: *God, if I'm really turning this situation over to you, I'm going to leave it there. I'm not going to worry about it. Thy will, not mine, be done.*

VICTORY IN PAIN

Because I hadn't cooperated with the government, I received an envelope. Inside was a newspaper article headlined: *"BLACK WIDOW."* The paper talked about my guilt and unwillingness to admit my wrongs. When I looked at the envelope, I saw that the D.A. had personally sent the article to me.

Over the coming days, I discovered the D.A. had also sent a copy to everyone who'd written a character letter on my behalf. On top of that, they made sure I was far away from my family; by the summer of 1994 I was sent to a high-security prison called Marianna Federal Correctional Institute in northern Florida.

I didn't know anything about Marianna. From the outside, it looked like any other prison I'd seen on TV. There were concrete walls, metal gates, and chain-link fences with razor wire twisted between them.

As soon as I was processed, I was taken to a unit

and introduced to the most enormous woman I'd ever seen. Her name was Miss Hannon and she was the unit manager.

"Welcome to Shawnee Unit," she told me. "You may live here, but this is my house. You may think having a life sentence is bad, but break one of my rules and it'll get worse!"

As I became familiar with the facility, I noticed it was different from the county jail: there were more activities. You could take different classes. You could work out and walk the track. The inmates were even allowed to do each other's hair and nails.

There was also a law library, where I was able to find out more about the system and how it operated. The first time I went to the law library I didn't know where to start. An inmate who worked there named Tanya was very helpful. I learned my security level was Low-In, which meant I could be transferred to a Low-In prison, a facility where you are fenced in.

I also learned there was a Low-In prison in Pleasanton, California. I went straight to Miss Hannon with what I'd discovered.

"Continue programming," she said. "Stay out of trouble, complete your required certifications, and work your job as the chapel clerk. Give me a clean year and I'll transfer you closer to home."

I had been an inmate companion and chapel clerk since I'd arrived at Marianna, witnessing and ministering, just as I had done before. If someone was having difficulty doing their time, I made myself available. I would pray and read Bible scripture with them. Squeaky Fromme, a member of the Manson Family, once told me: "You have a remarkable influence. Since you've been here, you've brought so much joy to this place."

I also ministered to a Colombian woman named Griselda Blanco. She had a fierce reputation. During our time in jail, I knew her to be a loving friend who regularly attended church. We often prayed together in my cell.

Just as she didn't talk about her life on the outside, I didn't talk about mine. It reminded me of what my older brother Johnny told me when I was first arrested.

"Don't talk about your life on the outside, just do your time. And if somebody messes with you, do what you have to."

Eventually, someone did.

A Puerto Rican woman named PJ asked, "Do you fool around with women?"

"NO!" I responded.

"I give you three years," she said. "You're pretty. Somebody's gonna turn you out."

I just walked away. But that wasn't the end of it.

The next day I had just finished my morning workout and was headed to my cell when PJ approached me again. This time she was aggressive.

"You think you're special or something?" she said, and shook her fist at me. "You know I like you. I like you a lot. And you're gonna like me too or you'll get some of this."

I looked in her clenched fist and noticed she had a jailhouse knife. I told her, "Okay. Whatever you want. Just put that thing up."

After she tucked it in her waistband, I socked her in the throat.

"If you ever approach me like that again," I yelled, "I'm going to shorten your life sentence!"

Then I walked away. I had two months left on my year. If I got busted for fighting, I wouldn't get my transfer.

That night in my cell, I thought about what I had done and prayed for PJ. I asked for forgiveness. God began to soften my heart. I had never felt this way about *anybody* who'd done something to me.

When my year was up, Miss Hannon made good on her word and transferred me to Pleasanton FCI near Oakland, California. It happened on July 28, 1995, Anthony's thirteenth birthday.

Pleasanton was bigger and had more facilities and classes. Most important, it was closer to home. Now my family could visit more frequently.

Anthony's first visit was a month later on my birthday. Hallelujah! I couldn't imagine a better present.

"All my friends skateboard," Anthony told me during our visit. "They laugh at me because I don't know how! They tell me I should stick to basketball!"

"Do you want to play basketball?" I asked.

"I want to skate!" he said. "And someday, I'm going to be really good! Right, Mommy?"

"That's right, baby," I told him. "You can do anything you set your mind to." Then I grabbed both his hands and began to pray: "God, bless my son and help him to be the best skateboarder!"

"Amen!" Anthony said.

After Anthony's visit, I was revitalized. I looked forward to seeing him once a month and on holidays. I also wanted to get transferred to the prison camp that was attached to Pleasanton FCI. To go to the FPC you had to have a Low-Out security level because there was no fence around it. I was still a Low-In, so I had to be inside a fence.

Every six months, I went up for evaluation before the unit team. My case manager, counselor, and unit manager was Miss Boynton. Every time I went to a team meeting, I came with all my certificates, proving that I was doing everything expected of me. I also worked hard at every job I was assigned.

Eventually, I went to work for Miss Boynton directly. It was a great work assignment and had many fringe benefits. Everybody wanted that job but she chose me. Some of the inmates were jealous but I didn't pay them any attention. I knew it was God's favor, so I focused on him instead and continued to minister.

God was really using me. He had positioned me where inmates *and* staff were approaching me for prayer.

At one point, I had a roommate who was disgusting. I told her several times: "You've got to wash your bed linens at least once a week and shower at least once a day," but she just would not do it!

One afternoon, she came in reeking from her job in the kitchen. I stared her down as she sat on her bunk but she ignored me.

"You are taking a shower!" I demanded.

"You ain't runnin' nothing!" she responded.

That was it. I lost it!

I told her, "Pack your stuff and get out!" after I finished beating on her. But instead of packing, she told the guards. That's how we both ended up in the hole.

The hole was isolation with one hour a day outside. At first I didn't understand—I knew I was there for fighting.

But why was I really there?

I didn't know, so I began to read every Christian book I could get my hands on. *The Desire of Ages* was the first book I read and it helped me to better understand the Bible. Next was *The Lady, Her Lover, and Her Lord* by T. D. Jakes, which encouraged me to keep seeking the Lord.

I read an entire book every two to five days. Those

books fed and nourished my heart. But next to the Bible, no book meant as much as Billy Graham's autobiography. His message of hope and salvation was strong, clear, and inspiring. If anyone has a connection with God, it's Billy Graham. Reading his book helped solidify my decision toward evangelistic ministry. This is when I accepted my calling from God. Doors began to open that only God himself could have opened.

After ninety days of investigation, there were no witnesses to the fight, so my old roommate and I were released. She was returned to the same unit. I was moved to a different one and assigned a new job as a weekend orderly. Now I only worked two days a week—God's favor once again.

By 1998 I was finally granted a transfer to Dublin Federal Prison Camp, which was part of a nearby army base. I was no longer in a lock-down facility. At the FPC, I had more freedom. It was a blessing to be at the camp.

Every morning after the 5:00 a.m. inmate count, I walked across camp to the chapel, prayed, and read my Bible. I also listened to praise and worship music.

I loved the healing message of CeCe Winans' beautiful song "Alabaster Box." When I listened to that song, I could feel God wrapping his arms all around me. The song lifted me out of the camp. I could feel God's presence. God never abandoned me. Everything I was going through was for his glory.

I also loved listening to Helen Baylor's testimony song, "Praying Grandmother." I had a praying grandmother. To hear her tell her testimony gave me hope that one day, I would tell mine.

And my faith grew stronger.

THE ONES I HURT

While on a visit in 1998 with my son, I could tell something was bothering him.

"What's the matter, baby?" I asked. "You feel okay?"

"I don't want to come here anymore," he told me. "I hate seeing you in this place!"

His words broke my heart. But I felt his pain on top of my own. The last thing I wanted to do was hurt my son. He didn't have a fifteen-year sentence—*I did!*—and I wasn't about to force him to come visit me any longer.

"I'm sorry," I told my son. "You don't have to visit if you don't want to." I prayed with him, we hugged and kissed, and he left.

Letting go of Anthony was one of the hardest things I had ever done. I cherished every moment we had spent together. I lived to see him grow from month to month. I had tried to talk to him about everything that was going on in his life, from school to friends to girls and how to be a gentleman.

Through our time together, I had also grown. I remembered back to years before, when Anthony asked, "Mom, can I tell my friend you're in jail?"

Up to that point, I'd told him it was nobody's business. But I could see this was important to him.

"Sure, baby."

On his next visit, his face was brighter than I'd seen it in a long time.

"My friend said his dad's in jail, too!"

Not having to keep my secret lightened his heart and formed a bond between Anthony and his friend.

When he asked me why I was in jail, I was straight with him. "For selling drugs," I said.

"Why did you do that?"

"Because I wanted to give you a better life," I told him. "I wanted you to have the best. But it was a mistake. It was the worst thing I could have done. I'm sorry."

I had mothered Anthony from jail the best I could. I saw to it that all his needs were met. I wrote him letters every day. He and I also kept a journal that we sent back and forth weekly. I called him every day. Whenever he got in trouble or got bad grades, I disciplined him.

But now he was sixteen and, like all sixteen-year-olds, was facing challenges of his own.

Around the same time he was becoming a man, the latter part of 1998, I was transferred to Twin Towers in downtown Los Angeles. It was not my choice.

Twin Towers was rough: uncomfortable and crowded. I was moved from floor to floor and never got to stay in any one place long.

Right after I was transferred, my mom and brother came to visit. My son wasn't with them.

I asked my mom, "How is Anthony doing?"

"He's fine," she said. "He's out skating."

I couldn't believe how much my son loved skating. I thought to myself: *How could skating be more important than coming to see me?*

After that visit, the prison staff continued to move me around. But once again, the Lord worked in mysterious ways. The more they moved me around, the more people I encountered in need of ministry. I had new opportunities to spread the word of God and less time to dwell on my own issues.

I began ministering to larger congregations. I made close contacts with prison staff and administration, not for the purpose of seeking special treatment, but to be of spiritual service. I became a prison trustee and spiritual adviser. I brought love to places where fear reigned and brought enemies together to worship in friendship. Even bully inmates who called the shots would come to me to lead nightly prayer groups.

One day, my counselor said, "There's a girl that needs your help."

Gina was a young woman who had just been diagnosed with cancer. Between facing a life sentence on her case and her illness, Gina was at a spiritual low point in her life.

"Do you have a relationship with God?" I asked.

"I was raised Catholic, but I haven't been to church in a while," she responded.

"Take my Bible for comfort," I offered, "and read it when your spirit is weak."

"Will Jesus heal this cancer?" she asked.

"Believe in him," I told her. "He brings eternal life in this world and the next to all those who have faith."

Gina and I became cell mates. I helped care for her. As she came to the Lord, she turned her life around. Even after Gina was transferred to the state prison in Chowchilla, we kept in contact through letters, even though we weren't allowed to write directly.

When she entered the terminal stages of her cancer, she was granted a compassionate release and sent home to be with her family. She was very weak so we would only speak briefly. Her mother always thanked me for calling. One day I called and Gina's mother told me, "My baby's not suffering anymore. She's gone to be with Jesus. I want you to know Gina never lost her faith."

Knowing that blessed me and touched my heart.

My experiences at Twin Towers continued to give my life purpose. My time there was the continuation of my journey. More and more, God began to show me his hand working in other people's lives.

An inmate named Michelle, who was facing twenty-five to life, came to me for prayer. God showed me that his plan for her was not imprisonment. I told her the day before her jury selection, "God says, 'Case dismissed.'"

Michelle went to court that morning and was released that afternoon.

It wasn't the only time I was shown God's will for others. Soon after God had spoken to me about Michelle, a prostitute facing three strikes came in for pulling a knife on a client. When she came to me, we spoke, and through God's guidance I saw a hung jury. Sure enough, that's exactly what happened.

God blessed me with the ability to be a light in a dark place.

When I finally transferred out of Twin Towers the summer of 2000, I wanted to go to Victorville FPC. It was even closer to home than Dublin, which was the new name for Pleasanton FCI. It was also a new place I could be of service to God and others. But my request was denied, so it was back to Dublin.

I didn't give up on Victorville, though. I put in for transfers and was denied each time. After two denials, I took it up with my case manager.

"Why can't I get to Victorville?"

"There's a separatist on you," she said.

"A *what*?" I asked.

"It keeps you apart from any codefendants on your

case that cooperated with the government." She meant *snitches.*

"Do you have any?" she continued.

"No," I told her. "They're all free."

She called the unit manager in Victorville and found out there *was* a separatist on me, a woman named Janine, who knew me from back in the day. The unit manager called Janine into her office while we waited on the phone.

"Do you have a problem with Jemeker Thompson coming here?" the unit manager asked Janine.

"Absolutely not!" Janine responded. "Tell her I want her to come. Jemeker needs to be closer to her son."

Once again, I was granted favor. My transfer was approved in 2001.

When I arrived at Victorville, Janine let me know: "The Feds came to me when you were on trial. They wanted me to testify against you. When I told them I didn't know you or your business, they told me to lie and said they'd cut my time if I did. But I wouldn't do it."

With tears in her eyes, we embraced. I started crying too—not just because the government conspired against me, but because if Janine had conspired with the government, I would have spent the rest of my life in prison.

I prayed and thanked God for blessing Janine with the strength to do the right thing. Then I thanked Janine and vowed:

"We are friends for life."

My time in Victorville was okay until one afternoon, while I was working in the laundry facility, when a male guard made an inappropriate advance on me. I stepped away from him and went about my business; I wasn't interested. But later that afternoon, he wrote a report, indicating that I had made the advance on *him*.

I was never given a chance to deny the charge; they just took me to the hole. But this time was different: I hadn't done anything to put myself there. So I knew it was God's will. I continued praying, reading, and writing.

I was in the hole for ninety days before they set a hearing for the charge I was given. It was my word against his, so you know how that turned out. I was found guilty and given an additional four months in the hole. As if that wasn't enough, they transferred me from the camp back to an FCI of their choice.

In the fall of 2002 when I returned to Dublin FCI and was getting settled back in, I learned about a drug diversion program offered by the prison system. Though I wasn't a drug addict—I had been addicted to the money that was generated by the drugs—the class was enlightening. I was able to hear the testimonies of people whose lives had been destroyed by the drugs I'd sold.

I'd never really thought about the harm and devastation I'd caused and I was remorseful. As soon as I felt remorse, it became clear to me why I had been sent to the hole.

After completing the program, there was a graduation ceremony. On November 5, 2003, when everyone received a certificate of completion, there was also another blessing—we all received a year off our sentences!

One afternoon, I was in the sports TV room when I happened to hear the ESPN commentator say, "Next up on the Vancouver Slam City Jam, pro skateboarder Anthony Mosley."

When I turned and looked up at the screen, I saw my baby.

Tears of joy rolled down my face as I screamed at the top of my lungs: *"Thank you Jesus for answering my prayer!"*

The sound of my scream brought the entire unit into the TV room. There he was—a pro skateboarder on television! We all watched in anticipation and cheered as he won Best Trick—*God had showed up and showed out once again!*

The following weekend I was in my cell when I heard my name over the PA system:

"THOMPSON, REPORT TO THE VISITING ROOM."

To my surprise, when I walked into the visiting room, Anthony was standing there. I ran and hugged him. He told me, "Take it easy, Mom! You're squeezing me too hard!"

"Sorry, but I can't help it," I replied. "I've missed you soooo much! Why didn't you tell me you were coming?"

"Well it's not like I could call you." He laughed. "Anyway, I wanted to surprise you!"

"Well you did! I was also surprised when I saw you on ESPN last weekend. Why didn't you tell me you were a pro skateboarder?"

"It's no big deal," he answered.

Right then, a young boy came over to ask Anthony for his autograph. After the youngster had broken the ice, all the older kids came over to our table and asked too.

I looked at Anthony and said, "It might not be a big deal to you but it sure is to everybody else!"

"It's just something I do!"

"Yes," I answered, "and you do it well!"

"Skating is my escape from reality, Mom. It's the only time I don't think about you being in this place."

The hardest part of my time was not being able to be there for my son. Once again, I felt my son's pain.

I fought back my tears as I said, "I'm soooo proud of you, baby. Hang in there; Mommy will be home soon."

DELIVERED . . . ?

I was thirty days to my release date from prison when another inmate disrespected me in the chow hall. She was much bigger than I was and knew I didn't want to lose my release date for fighting. When I ignored her, she got louder.

"I'm through talking!" she yelled. "Come to my cell and we can handle this right now!"

Everyone in the chow hall was trying to egg it on with their *oooooos* and *ahhhhhhs*. But I didn't feed into it.

Later that day, Big Girl got off work. As she walked into her cell, I came in right behind her. The way she had talked to me in the chow hall had opened up a can that I tried my best to keep closed. When I was finished teaching Big Girl some respect, I let her know:

"This is between me and you. I'm not trying to lose my release date. I'm sure you're not trying to lose yours. I'm not saying a word—you make sure you do the same!"

The very next morning after the 5:00 a.m. count, I was taken to the Special Housing Unit; someone had seen the bruises on Big Girl and had dropped a note to the guards. When they asked me what had happened, I pleaded the fifth. Big Girl didn't tell them anything either, so I didn't lose my date. They let her out of the SHU after a week, but kept me there, which was actually a favor, because who knows what could have happened if they'd allowed me to return to the yard.

FINALLY!

February 18, 2005. 8:00 a.m., I was released from the hole.

But this time was different. I had served my full sentence with the exception of one year off for completing the drug program.

I knew I was looking at the inside of those walls for the last time. As I was walked across the yard, people were cheering and waving good-bye. After I changed into street clothes that had been sent to me by a friend, I was processed out!

As I walked through the front door of Dublin FCI, I thanked God for delivering me and protecting me through my trials. I was driven to the train station and dropped off.

A dear friend of mine, Sherry, picked me up. We hugged, prayed, and thanked God. Then she asked me, "Where do you want to eat breakfast, sister?"

"House of Pancakes," I answered.

As we got on the freeway, I couldn't help but notice how fast the cars were moving; I hadn't seen a car on the freeway in a long time. I was accustomed to functioning in prison parameters. I was used to everything moving slow.

When we got to IHOP I ordered a glass of milk, a small orange juice, buttermilk pancakes with hot maple syrup, turkey sausages, and scrambled eggs with cheese and onions.

"That was the best food I've had in twelve years!" I told Sherry.

After breakfast, Sherry gave me the agenda. "We're getting manicures and pedicures. Then we're going shopping at the mall."

Being pampered at the nail salon felt like a dream. Afterward, we went to Macy's. When we got there, Sherry said, "Get whatever you want!"

I was overwhelmed. I was used to shopping from a piece of paper, marking numbers next to items, not even being able to see what I was purchasing. Besides, I really didn't want anything. But Sherry insisted and started handing me the things she thought I needed.

The last thing on my mind was shopping. The only thing I could think about was getting home to my family.

When my plane landed in Los Angeles, there was a handsome twenty-two-year-old waiting for me at the curb. I ran to my baby, who was now a grown man, grabbed him in my arms, and hugged him. We were so excited, neither one of us could stop smiling.

As Anthony drove to my mother's house, I noticed L.A. had changed quite a bit. When we arrived at Mom's, the family was there to greet me.

"How'd you stay so young?" my aunt asked. "What's your secret?"

"It's no secret," I told her. "God preserved me. All honor, glory, and praise go to him! If it was not for the Lord, I would have lost my mind!"

"Amen!" she said.

As much as I was enjoying my family, I had to leave. I was supposed to report straight to the halfway house. At least I got to see my mother first.

I checked in at the halfway house, which was in El Monte, California. They explained the rules: you couldn't leave the house without a pass. The only way you were given a pass was if you were going to work or looking for work. To stay in the halfway house, you had to get a job. If you didn't get a job, you went back to jail. When you weren't at work or looking for work, you were given chores.

The chores were easy. Looking for work? Not so easy. I filled out application after application and interviewed constantly but was never hired. It was discouraging.

Slipping back into my old life was not an option. I

was nice to everyone who came to see me at the halfway house. But I was also clear about my new direction.

"Whenever you're ready to do business, I'm with you," said a former colleague.

"I can't do that anymore," I replied. "I'm serving Jesus now."

"Wow," he said. "I heard you were an evangelist. That's cool." Before he left, he handed me a roll of money with a rubber band around it. "If you change your mind, call me!"

No sooner than I had passed that test, I was faced with another one. A friend I hadn't seen since I'd been arrested came to visit. When we stepped out on the patio, she whispered:

"I know where Cheez is. Do you want me to handle it?"

"No," I told her. "I'm a Christian now. I forgave him a long time ago."

I knew the tests were not over. Not only did I need to find a job, but a covenant as well. I reached out to a prominent pastor of the church where I was once a member. I left several messages. To my surprise, I never received a response from anyone.

I wrestled with myself not to condemn the pastor. I prayed and fasted for three days. At the end of my fast, God told me to go hear the pastor preach. So I did.

When I arrived at the church, the pastor was preaching from the book of Genesis 32:22–32. The title of the sermon was "Bless Me."

He talked of Jacob, disguised as his brother, Esau, asking his father Isaac to bless him. I saw myself in Jacob, looking for blessings from God. As he preached, he left the pulpit, went into the congregation and began laying hands. I had never seen him do this.

He touched four people, and before I knew it, he was standing in front of me. I was the last person he touched before he returned to the pulpit.

The moment he laid hands on me and said, "Bless her, Lord," I understood that the messenger is only human, but the message is divine. I felt the power of God's love strengthening my faith.

The next Sunday, I joined my friend Sonya's church, where her husband was pastor. In this loving congregation, I felt completely accepted. I told my pastor:

"My halfway house requires that I get a job. I've been having challenges finding one. But I know God has called me to minister."

I soon began to minister everywhere. My speaking engagements flourished and I was receiving love offerings from other congregations.

God had given me a job.

MORE THAN A CONQUEROR

My friend Sumer had come to visit me at the halfway house. I was ministering to her when I was interrupted by my case manager, who told me to come to her office after the visit. On my way there I wondered what was so important that she had to interrupt my visit. When I got to her office, she told me: "I have good news. Your records indicate that you have ninety days' clear conduct, which makes you eligible to receive home confinement for your remaining ninety days. You need to have a residence and a landline phone without three-way calling and you must be in no later than nine p.m." I hugged and thanked my case manager and went to the phone and called my son, Anthony, to share the good news. I also asked him to move in with me and he said he would. Not only was I getting out of the halfway house, but my baby was moving in with me. I was so overjoyed. I got off the phone went to my room and started packing. That night I couldn't sleep. The next morning, I left the halfway house in search of a two-bedroom apartment. I filled out an application for the first apartment I looked at. I was approved and given keys. I moved that day. I didn't have much to move from the halfway house. But when I went to the storage space that had been occupied with my belongings for twelve years, that was a different story. I knew there was no way all this would fit in my two-bedroom apartment. *Going through all those old things let me know just how long I'd been away.* I took out what I needed and gave the rest to the Salvation Army. The move took all day—but I made sure I was in the house by 9:00 p.m. I didn't want any problems. I was looking forward to taking a warm bubble bath—something I hadn't done in twelve years. *There were no tubs in prison or the halfway house.* I felt good to be in my own place. That night I slept like a baby. The next morning I got up and cooked; the smell of the sizzling bacon woke up Anthony. We had our first breakfast together in our new home. I enjoyed cooking all his favorites. We'd laugh, talk, and watch movies together.

Before I knew it three months had passed. I told Anthony I was no longer on home confinement.

"What! You don't have to be in by nine anymore? We have to celebrate, Mom, come to the club with me tonight," he responded.

"I'd love to hang out with you, but I don't do clubs anymore," I said.

"Well, you have to do something. Please don't sit in the house all night."

"Maybe I'll go skating."

"Skating! Hmm, that sounds fun."

"You want to go?" I asked him.

"No—I already have plans. Maybe I'll go with you some other time."

"Are you coming home tonight?" I asked him.

"No—I'll be back next week," he told me.

Even though Anthony moved in with me he still had his own place in the city. After Anthony left I called some friends and let them know I was coming to the skating rink. Word got around that I'd be there; when I arrived, people I hadn't seen in years showed up to welcome me home.

As I slipped on my skates, I listened to the DJ play the Gap Band's "Yearning for Your Love," and the S.O.S. Band's "Weekend Girl." Those old songs took me back. All around me, couples linked arms and rolled with style. They skated to the music, crossing their legs and bouncing to the beat. I rolled out onto the floor a little unsteady—it had been twelve years since I'd skated—but I put one foot in front of the other and started moving.

A few minutes later, I heard a familiar voice behind me.

"Jemeker!"

When I turned around, there was Champ. He was a little older, but handsome as ever.

"I heard you were coming tonight," he said.

Champ took me by the arm and we rolled together for the rest of the night.

"Let me take you to breakfast," Champ said after the DJ played the last song. I was happy to say yes.

"How's life outside?" Champ asked.

"Still getting used to everything," I admitted. "But God is good. He protects and keeps me every day."

"When I got out, I had to learn to shop at the grocery store," he said. "Too many choices. I was used to the commissary sheet they gave us back in prison where we hardly had any choice at all."

I laughed and admitted I had a similar reaction. We talked about how he'd done ten years for the same thing as me. We had a lot in common.

"When I got to jail, I was angry and bitter," Champ told me. "For the first two years, I didn't program; man, I *lived* in the hole. But one day, an OG who was a friend of my uncle's pulled me to the side and said, 'Youngster, do the time. Don't let the time do you.' He was a Muslim and said Islam had helped him."

"The power of God was the only thing that could clean me up," I said.

"I wasn't trying to hear about religion, though," Champ added. "All I ever saw in religion was people claiming to be one thing but doing something else. So my uncle's friend sent for the prison imam. He came to see me in the hole. When I tried to argue scripture with him, he always beat me down, but never lost his cool. He had a peace to him. I wanted that peace. When I got out of the hole, the imam gave me a job in the chapel. I learned the prayers and prayed five times a day. Becoming a Muslim gave me discipline and turned me around."

"Did it give you peace?" I asked.

"I wasn't as angry," he admitted. "It kept me out of the hole and made me watch what I said. I also started programming. I told my mom I was Muslim and she was not pleased. 'I raised you a Christian!' she exclaimed.

"But when she came to visit, she said, 'I don't know what you're doing in here, but it's working for you.' That's when I started to see how a power greater than myself was making a difference in my life."

I told Champ about how I had a relationship with Christ. He listened. That night at Denny's we talked until 5:00 in the morning.

"You know what's funny?" Champ said at the end of our date. "I wasn't going to come skating tonight. I changed my mind when I heard you were going to be there, but I was still expecting the old Jemeker."

"She's gone." I laughed.

"I can tell," he said. "You've got a glow I've never seen before. I want to see you again."

"I'd like to see you again too," I told Champ, "but

I'm not looking for a casual relationship. That was the old Jemeker."

"Well, I'm not looking for a casual relationship either," Champ told me. "I want to get to know the new Jemeker."

When we parted company that morning, Champ told me to call him if I got lost. Secretly, I hoped that I would. Sure enough, I took a wrong turn, and when I called Champ, he talked me all the way home.

No doubt about it, I liked Champ. But when I thought about him in a romantic way, I wondered if I could love a man whose faith was different from mine. I went to my pastor and asked his advice. To my surprise, he encouraged me to date Champ.

"Islam has opened the door for Champ to see the power of God," he told me.

"I'm attracted to this man," I explained to my pastor, "but he's not the type of person who can be told what to think, especially when it comes to God. He needs proof."

"When he sees the evidence of your transformation in Christ, you won't have to tell him anything. He'll believe his own eyes."

Over the next few months, Champ and I dated. We were exclusive. We built a relationship based on spiritual intimacy, not physical intimacy. It wasn't always easy. No matter how late it was, Champ always went home instead of spending the night.

We also practiced an honest exchange of information and didn't play mind games. We learned each other's likes and dislikes, hopes and dreams, and talked openly about our pasts.

Old-fashioned courtship was a new experience for both of us. But we could see the quality of the relationship that was building. We talked about God all the time. And just like he had seen Jesus's light inside me the first night we were together, I began to see that light in him.

Champ wasn't the only one who changed. I had always been afraid of roller coasters when Champ took me to Magic Mountain one summer's day. As we waited to ride the Colossus—a giant wooden beast—I began to get a headache. The closer we came to the front of the line, the faster my heart began to pump. By the time we were about to board I was terrified.

"You can do this," Champ said. "I'll be right there beside you."

I didn't want to get on that roller coaster but I did. Champ made sure we were sitting in the very front. There was nothing in front of us but track.

"Open your eyes, baby," he told me as we climbed into the sky. "You can do this!"

As soon as we got to the top of the first drop, I *did* face my fears head-on! I had no choice! I screamed as we dropped hundreds of feet through the air! I hung on to Champ's hand for dear life as we swooped around the corners and went up and down, over and over again! The whole time, I prayed.

But as we rode, I noticed my screams turning to laughter. When I looked at Champ, he was smiling. I could feel the corners of my mouth and I was smiling too!

I was having fun!

Champ was right; there was nothing to be afraid of. When it was over, I turned to him and said, "Can we go again?" then turned to God and said, *Thank you for putting this man in my life to help me conquer my fears.*

Champ took me out every night. One evening, we went for a romantic dinner. Everything was perfect, from the delicious food to the glowing candles. As we ate our meal, though, I looked across the table and could see something troubling him.

"Baby, what's wrong?" I asked.

"We've known each other for a while now," Champ said. "And we keep moving in a positive direction. I want to take us to the next level."

"I do too." I smiled.

"I've been watching your relationship with Jesus for months. I see the peace and calmness it brings you and I want to share your faith."

"I want to share Jesus with you too," I said. "I want to help lead you to a more intimate relationship with God. But what's troubling you?"

"I still have doubt," he told me. "If God's performing miracles in my life, I need him to give me a sign."

I admired his courage for admitting that to me. I also thought back to my own experience: How many times had I asked God to show me signs, yet still doubted his presence? Right up to the morning I was baptized, I was still asking for a sign of my own. So I said, "Whenever you're ready to receive Christ, I will lead you in the Sinner's Prayer."

"I'm ready now," he said.

When we got to my house, I began to pray with Champ. I asked him to admit he was a sinner and to believe that Jesus is Lord, and that night Champ received Christ.

As I prayed, Champ began speaking in tongues but stopped abruptly.

"Baby, what's wrong?" I asked.

"I don't want to speak," he said, "if I don't know what I'm saying."

Champ was still resistant, but I knew better than to rush him in his own spiritual experience.

"You'll know when the time is right," I reassured him. After he left that night, I said another prayer before I went to sleep: *Please God, give Champ interpretation.*

"It happened!" Champ exclaimed when I saw him the next morning. "I was in the shower and the Holy Spirit came over me! Only this time, I knew what I was saying!"

"What did God show you?" I asked.

"My sins," he told me. "Then he showed me his mercy and forgiveness!"

It was a blessing!

Champ had an encounter with God!

One night, on our way home from dinner, Champ took me back to the Denny's where we'd had our first date.

"What are we doing here?" I asked. "We already ate."

"I have a friend I want you to meet," he said.

Brian, who was waiting inside, turned out to be a jeweler from Chino Hills. When he opened the locked briefcase he carried with him, it was full of diamonds, gold, platinum, and custom jewelry. As Champ tried on watches and bracelets, he said:

"Baby, why don't you pick out a ring that you like?"

I chose a small but tasteful platinum-and-diamond band. The jeweler had fancier rings with larger stones, but they were unnecessary; the one I selected fit me perfectly.

Soon after, I flew to Houston to meet Champ's mother. I had gotten to know her over the phone, but our connection in person was special, right from the moment we met.

I came to know Champ's mother as a woman of powerful faith and intelligence. She was a prayer warrior. We shared knowledge of the Bible together and worshipped and prayed together. She made sure her family welcomed me with open arms.

"Jemeker, I just want to thank you for leading my son to Jesus."

By now, Champ and I had been dating for over

a year. We had spent every day together. We'd shared every meal. I knew all there was to know about him and he knew everything about me.

"I asked my mom what she thought," Champ said one afternoon after we got home. "She said, 'That's my daughter.' You already know how I feel about you."

With that, Champ got on one knee and took my hands in his.

"Baby," he continued, looking in my eyes, "please be my wife. I want to spend the rest of my life with you."

"Yes!" I cried.

I would have been crazy to say no!

In Champ, I saw all the wonderful qualities that every woman would want in a man. I felt Champ's love, joy, kindness, and gentleness. He was a man after God's own heart and my soul mate.

We left Houston as Mr. and Mrs. Hairston. I was one of the happiest women in the world. God had answered my prayer.

SECOND CHANCE

It's Wednesday, December 31, and I'm relaxing in a nice, warm bubble bath.

My mind and spirit are at peace. I'm in a cozy condominium near the Hollywood Hills where Champ and I now live. We've also been led to a new church in Stevenson Ranch, California. The first time we attended, there were only a few members. Now we have close to three hundred and it's only been nine months. Valencia Christian Center is a loving congregation of people from all races, creeds, and walks of life. Marlon Saunders is the pastor and a great example of what a minister should be.

I dress, pray, and drive to church. On the way, Champ and I laugh about how we used to bring in New Year's. We were never thankful, just wild. Now we're filled with gratitude to God for giving us another year.

When we arrive, I'm excited; there's no greater joy

than to be used by God and I can feel he's getting ready to use me.

Before I begin, I pray:

Let the words of my mouth and the meditation of my heart be pleasing to you, Lord. May I decrease as you increase; let your people look past the messenger and receive the message. In Jesus's name, Amen.

When my prayer is finished, I begin.

"It's the end of the year and today is a victory celebration. This is my personal testimony. Let me tell you who I used to be:

"A backslider.

"Bitter and afraid.

"A liar.

"Doubting, worried, prideful, angry, and hurt.

"An adultress.

"Deceitful, fearful, judging, and controlling.

"A gossiper.

"A murderer.

"A slanderer.

"A complainer.

"A cheater.

"A thief.

"A manipulator.

"A lover of money and clothes.

"A fighter.

"A drug dealer.

"If I left anything out, only God knows. I want you

to know today that God is the only one who cleaned me up. I don't look, feel, or behave anything like who I used to be. It's his love and joy that lives in me and his grace and mercy that helps me get through each and every day.

"1 John 2:15: *Do not love the world or the things of the world. If anyone loves the world, the love of the Father is not in him.*

"I'm a witness of his glory. I was married to one of the biggest drug dealers in L.A. I was no stranger to the drug underworld. My husband was killed at a very young age but that did not stop me. I continued dealing drugs.

"I opened a company selling Italian hair to launder money. I supplied men in Atlanta, Miami, Detroit, St. Louis, and L.A. It was all about the money.

"1 Timothy 6:10: *For the love of money is the root of all kinds of evil.* I wanted only name-brand everything and would not want anyone in my world that I felt was not on my level.

"An ex-boyfriend got busted and was looking at a life sentence. He gave me up in exchange for his freedom. I'd always said they'd have to kill me before I turned myself in, so I went on the run until I was arrested in front of my son at his sixth-grade graduation.

"I had never been to prison and was looking at twenty-five to life. I was found guilty and served twelve years.

"Isaiah 43:25: *I, even I, am He who blots out your transgressions for my own sake, and I will not remember your sins.*

"God allowed me to be broken so I could see his plan.

"Today I am an anointed woman of God and the founder of Second Chance Evangelist Ministries.

"Because God gave me a second chance, I wanted to be a positive influence to women via written correspondence while incarcerated, or anyone who needs spiritual support. If I can touch just one person's heart, my mission has been accomplished.

"It doesn't matter what you have gone through. You, too, can have Jesus, for in him is victory. He also has a plan and purpose for each and every one of you, just keep on seeking him.

"God will still use you if you want to be used."

After the service, I'm surrounded by people hugging me and shaking my hand. As one lady tells me my testimony really blessed her, another hands me a folded piece of paper with her daughter's name, booking number, and address.

"Will you write to her?" she asks. "She needs to be encouraged."

"Sure," I say. "That's what God has called me to do."

When I think about the goodness of the Lord, I'm overcome with a feeling of love and humility. He has taken a sinner like me and changed me into a servant for him.

Revelations 12:11: *And they overcame him by the blood of the lamb and by the word of their testimony; and they loved not their lives unto death.*

To God be the glory.

THE BEGINNING

ACKNOWLEDGMENTS

I wish to thank my mother, Lonnie Johnson, for being the best mother that she could be. Your love, support, and encouragement have been consistent. Mom, without you, there would be no me. Thank you for my exposure to Christ at an early age. Experiencing some of your struggles with you has enabled me to stand strong during the storm.

Thank you to my three princes: Anthony M. Mosley, you are a great joy to me and I thank God for your Angel that continues to protect you; and my two sons through marriage, Kevin Hairston, who could not be loved more if biological, and Rodney Jamil (RJ) Hairston, who is far away but ever close in our hearts.

To Eera (Sumer) West, you spent tireless months, days, and hours writing, reading, correcting, and rewriting this manuscript, along with my husband, Champ. You are truly one of my dearest friends.

Thank you to my closest friends, Evangelist Tynia Dean, Anita Kaufman, Sonya Morgan Charles, Marcia Turner, Robin Cash, and Sherry Galarsa. These ladies helped to push me toward my destiny. There is no greater blessing than to be surrounded by true friends who know who you really are *and* are willing to let you be you!

My spiritual mothers: Pastor Cassandra Steptoe, Pastor Dorothy Evans, Pastor Rosalind Bunett, Pastor Eloise Carey, Jean Hayward, Dorothy Anderson, Ann Williams, and Carlynn Fanning. Thank you for your prayers, counsels, and never-ending encouragement.

To my mother-in-law, Nina Goins, who I call Mom, for accepting me as your daughter, not "in-law." Thank you for being a believer of the Word that "if you pray for your children, God will save them" (Isa 49:24). Your prayers in asking God to send someone to your son whom he would listen to opened the door for me to be instrumental in leading him to Christ. Praise God!

My brothers, Johnny Johnson, Fernando Thompson, Clifton Butts and my sister, Priscilla Thompson.

My grandsons, Yoshi Blaine Yoshihama and Carter Anthony Mosley.

My in-laws, Kenneth and Glenda Hairston, Terry and Stephenie Mack, Todd and Rocelle Hairston, NiDon Goins, Rochelle Mason, and Loretta Johnson. Thank you for loving me as family.

My pastor, Marlon Saunders, and First Lady Tamara

Saunders, and the Valencia Christian Center church family. Thank you for the love, support, and prayers that you have showered on me.

Gobi M. Iranian, who made it possible for me to obain my book deal by making my DVD. Thank you for your time and effort.

A special thanks to actor Wren Brown, for coming into my life and believing in my vision of bringing *Queen Pin* to life. I can never repay you for your positive feedback.

Thank you, Karen R. Thomas, executive editor of Grand Central Publishing, for your belief in me, which pushed me to another level.

My lawyer, Jeff Siberman, thank you for having faith in me and my dream. I love you so much.

My manager, Barry Krost.

My literary agent, David Vigliano of Vigliano Associates.

My writers, David Ritz and Geoff Martin.

My doctors, Laurence Bruksch and Carla E. Herriford.

And, finally, my first husband, Anthony M. (Daff) Mosley, whose presence in my earlier life was instrumental in the birth of *Queen Pin*.